CLEAR CHANGE

CLEAR CHANGE

The Executive's Guide to Leading Transformations that Stick

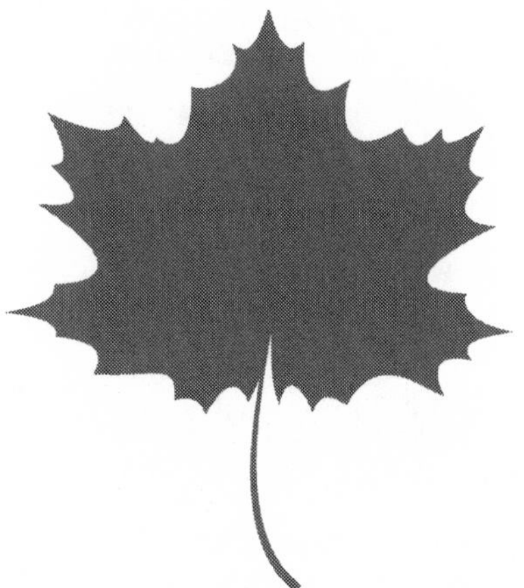

Alison P. Spoonmore

CLEAR Change: the Executive's Guide to Leading Transformations that Stick

ISBN (paperback): 978-1-7375109-0-1
ISBN (ebook): 978-1-7375109-1-8

Library of Congress Control Number: 2021913098

FREE GUIDEBOOK!

Connect with us at CLEARChangeBook.com
for your free CLEAR Change Guidebook

Ready to start? Follow along as you read CLEAR Change. Use the tools and templates to map your change journey, creating lasting positive change.

If you'd like to connect with us,
do so through our website:

www.CLEARChangeBook.com

To Bob, who fills each day with love and laughter.

I'm so happy to be on this adventure with you!

TABLE OF CONTENTS

INTRODUCTION

I love stories with humor, snappy dialogue, and complex characters. The most impactful stories share palpable struggles and eventual resolutions, taking the audience along on a journey. With the best of these movies, we are Changed. Motivated. Inspired.

In business, we are enthralled by stories of great leaders who take the world by storm, creating tremendous value, disrupting the status quo, and occasionally changing the world for good. With the best of these stories, we are Changed. Motivated. Inspired.

We herald these stories of success, applying their proven approach to our own businesses in the hopes the recipe will produce success for us. But it isn't as easy as it seems; in fact, 70 percent of all change initiatives fail. You read that right, more than 70 percent do not produce the desired results! (Kotter 2012). The application of someone else's business model has a high probability of failure, but if we cannot apply what others have learned, how are we to improve? Is it just luck?

Fortunately, there is a way to define and ***drive your own journey*** that does not rely on a stroke of luck. To succeed and grow your business, you must define and apply specific changes, intentionally, guided by an organized roadmap of defined processes and experiences. The path forward is CLEAR, once you map your destination. Driving change is much easier on a well-charted course.

This book is for you, regardless of your position—as a change leader, a team member, an influential leader, or an employee in a changing business environment. At the core, success comes when people invest in the vision of the future, however great or moderate the target. Change starts with you!

How to Read this Book

The CLEAR Change Method provides a map for your change journey, but like any navigation system, there are multiple routes that can get you from here to there. With that in mind, we've created multiple reading options. Choose the route that best fits your navigation preferences.

Traditional Approach—Front to Back

For those who cannot conceive of flipping pages, I encourage you to read this book front to back. You will experience three parables, each derived from real change initiatives, but presented with woodland creatures in the leading roles. The inhabitants of the Clover Meadow face real threats, each mapping a change journey with differing issues and outcomes. Each parable includes discussion sections to explain and explore the elements of the CLEAR Change Method. Engaging your team in reading and discussing each parable will support understanding of the method and promote discussion specific to your change initiative.

Once you've read and discussed the parables in Section 1, you can move forward to Section 2 for a more technical presentation of the CLEAR Change Method. Each chapter includes definitions, application tools, pitfalls, and case studies. With the technical explanation of each element, you can apply the method to your change initiative. The parables provide the overview, preparing you and your team for the more detailed application. If that sounds good to you, the front-to-back approach is a good map for your journey toward successful implementation.

Another Approach—The Last Shall be First

For those of you who cannot possibly suffer through cute yet meaningful stories of woodland creatures, I invite you to fast forward to Section 2. Here you will find a more technical exploration of the CLEAR Change Method, complete with tools, definitions, pitfalls, and case studies. It's not as much fun, but it is complete and straightforward (as any process should be). Once you've learned the method, I invite you to read the parables and delight in your new-found knowledge, having all the answers for your team's discussion!

The Third Approach—The Sandwich Option

A unique book calls for a unique approach! Like a good club sandwich, enjoy the CLEAR Change Parables in layers.

Layer 1: Parable 1 provides an overview of the CLEAR Change Method, well constructed and applied.

Layer 2: Technical chapters C is for Contrast and L is for Leadership provides insights on the method, tools, and pitfalls.

Layer 3: Parable 2 shows how change initiatives may be derailed if Contrast and Leadership are not aligned.

Layer 4: Technical chapters E is for Experiences and A is for Accountability outline engagement and ownership, the engine of the change journey.

Layer 5: Parable 3 shows how the pitfalls in Experiences and Accountability impact the change initiative.

Layer 6: The last chapter, R is for Reinforcement, and then Parable 1 again. This will reinforce successful application. It all comes together like a great sandwich!

Read the book how it best suits your needs, and engage your team as you see fit. Even in business, change is personal—map your journey and lead the way!

SECTION 1

The CLEAR Change Parables

"As long as you keep one foot in the real world while the other foot's in a fairy tale, that fairy tale is going to seem kind of attainable."

—Aaron Sorkin, screenwriter

The CLEAR Change Parables document real change initiatives, messy in reality yet simple to understand when presented in the magical world of the Clover Meadow. To understand the real-world process, the parables will require you to place one foot into the fairy tale, as Sorkin suggested. The characters represent leaders, influencers, and participants; they include change leaders, mentors, followers, resisters, well-meaning experts, and maybe not-so-well-meaning challengers. You may see yourself in the parable, you may notice your boss, your colleagues. The stories are familiar, depicting successes, challenges, and failures inherent in any change journey.

To orient you on your journey, the CLEAR Change Method is comprised of five key elements:

C = Contrast	**Define the change to be realized,** compare your current state to the desired future state, and articulate the value of the change (From This, To That, and Why) This is the core of the change initiative, influencing every other element and phase of the journey
L = Leadership	**Engage leaders**—both formal and informal—into the need to change and the value to be realized
E = Experiences	**Architect experiences for all** leaders, doers, and users that introduce the change and define how we might make it easy to do the new thing the right way. This is the biggest factor in the change journey!
A = Accountability	**Establish clear roles and ownership** for the planned actions and outcomes. This element ensures execution of Experiences and progress along the journey.
R = Reinforcement	**Reinforce the desired outcomes** and celebrate interim successes and progress toward the finish line. Remembering and recognizing the milestones along the journey of change helps individuals accept and adopt the new normal, sustaining the desired change.

Guided discussion sections are presented as follows:

- **Decoding the Parable** explores elements of the CLEAR Change Method, highlighting points of interest throughout the parable. Discussion of each element will help you understand the parable and the method, as well as prepare for application.
- **Discussion Questions** explore deeper points that follow or fail to follow the method for successful change. I provide responses for your consideration, but not an exhaustive set of answers. This section is well-suited for team-based discussion and learning.
- **Application Questions** translate the lessons from the parable into your specific change initiative. Similar to a book club, a guided discussion prompts new insights on what you've read. There are no provided answers for these questions, as they are for use with *your* team in *your* context.

Let's begin the journey of change with a story.

PARABLE 1

The Knight, the Doe, and the Duck

Once upon a time, there was a brave Knight. Although still young, the Knight was kind, patient, optimistic, and brave. The Knight was returning to the Castle and walked through the forest quietly, chatting politely to the animals and whistling gently to the cardinals above. The path was wide, and the Knight tripped along, unaware of the danger gathering behind.

The Knight was jubilant, having recently vanquished a dragon in the dark recesses of the kingdom. The victor skipped along, listening to the clang of the armor with each step. The epic journey to the dragon's lair, the bravery of facing the dragon, and slaying the beast among fire and talons of steel—this was the stuff of legend! The Knight was eager to return home to recount the triumph in story and song.

Then, a Doe appeared in the path. The Knight stopped whistling and drew breath in surprise. The Doe was visibly distressed, looking back along the path and to the Knight with wide eyes.

"You must hurry, young Knight! They are soon upon us!"

"Who?"

"The Wolves. They will destroy you! You must hurry to the Castle and warn the others!"

The Doe and the Knight moved through the woods as quickly as the Knight could travel; the armor was protective in times of peril, but could be cumbersome when speed was necessary.

"Dear Doe, I am moving as fast as I can, but I fear I am tired. Why must we move so quickly? I can't see any Wolves..."

"Dear Knight, did I not share with you how hungry and destructive the Wolves can be? I have seen many villages ravaged by their gnashing teeth and slashing claws! We must rush to protect the kind people who live in your Village!"

The Doe leaped forward on the path, out of the woods, across a meadow of fragrant clover to the bank of a raging river. The Knight followed soon after, breathing heavily above the roar of the tumultuous rapids.

"We must cross the river," said the Doe.

"I cannot! The water is too deep to wade across, and the rapids are too difficult to navigate. I will not be able to keep my footing! We must build a bridge; that is what we have done at the Castle. If only we had a few people to help us, and some stones to create the towers …"

"We do not have the time for towers and bridges! We must swim across."

"I do not swim," the Knight said with finality.

At that time, a Fish was swimming by and overheard the conversation.

"Swimming is easy!" the Fish offered. "I am an expert swimmer!"

"Of course swimming is easy, for a Fish. How do you do it?" asked the Knight.

"I've never really thought about describing how to swim, but I will try. You just move your tail from side to side to move forward, and you change direction with your fins. And do not forget to breathe through your gills." The Fish was very confident in his description, sure that anyone who had been in the water would understand the clear and concise directions.

"I don't have fins or gills!" the Knight yelled in frustration. The Doe continued to look behind them, listening for footsteps of impending doom.

"Thank you for your kind assistance" the Doe said to the Fish, nodding in appreciation. "But I think we need a different answer." She turned back to the Knight. "We must find another teacher. I know of a Duck who may help us. Follow me!"

The Doe bounded off toward a path on the edge of the woods, away from the raging river.

"Thank you, and goodbye!" said the Knight to the Fish, following closely behind the Doe.

How on earth could a Duck help?

The Knight caught up to the Doe at the edge of a clear pond. The Doe was drinking gently, gazing across the water. A Duck glided across the surface of the pond, quacking a greeting to the stately Doe.

"Hello, Dear Doe! How wonderful of you to visit!"

"Hello, Dear Duck! I am happy to see you and to ask for your help."

The Duck nodded, exchanged pleasantries with the Knight, and listened to the Doe explain the urgent necessity to teach the Knight how to cross the river.

"The best way to learn is by doing," said the Duck. "You must get into the water here in the pond, where the water is shallow and calm. You must remove your armor so you will not sink!"

Leaving the armor on the shore concerned the Knight, even though the Duck's reasoning was sound. The Doe assured the Knight the armor would be safe.

The Knight soon stepped into the pond, with the cool water lapping just under the arms.

"The trick is to spread out your body on the surface, like a log that has fallen into the river and floats with the current."

The Duck first demonstrated with a small stick, then showed the Knight how her body and feathers floated on the top of the water.

The Knight laid out in the water, face down, flailing as the water covered the face.

"This will not work; I will surely die from lack of air!"

"You must keep your head up," offered the Doe. "It is challenging when you are still but works well when you are moving forward."

The Knight was skeptical.

"If you know how to cross the river, why can't you carry me across?" asked the Knight. "You're sturdy and strong. It would certainly be faster than learning how to swim."

"I cannot carry you across," she said with certainty. "The current will carry us down the rapids and over the waterfall before we reach the opposite shore."

"Waterfall?" The Knight had not noticed the waterfall with the worry about the rapids and the Wolves on the path. "What's next?"

The Duck showed the Knight how paddling with her feet not only moved her forward but also helped with direction. Gracefully completing a circle, the Duck looked at the Knight with confidence and positivity.

"You have hands *and* feet! You have twice the ability to move and steer as I do!"

Buoyed by her confidence, the Knight glided forward into the water, head up, moving arms and legs with rapid fluttering to stay afloat.

After a moment, the Knight shouted, "There is no rest! I am already tired!"

"Move in a rhythm, as if running on a path," said the Doe, "and move your arms as if they are front legs spread wide."

The Knight deliberately took in calming breaths and tried again, completing a few circles. It wasn't so hard, especially when knowing the opportunity to stand up in the shallow water was available.

"It is time to cross the river," said the Doe anxiously. "You are ready."

"Surviving the pond is easy; I'm not ready to fight the rapids. Especially not in my armor!"

"The rapids are not an issue," offered the Duck. "I know a place where the current is gentle, but the river is deep and wide. It will take all your strength to cross as you are, without your armor. You must leave it behind."

The armor was part of the Knight's identity, bestowed by the King, certainly essential for protection in the business of slaying dragons. The Knight fumbled with the visor on the helmet, reluctant to leave it behind.

"There are no dragons in the river." The Doe was resolute.

"I must carry my sword; it is my only defense if the Wolves overtake us." The Knight was not quite sure the Doe understood the risks of a Knight without armor.

"Let us lash it to your back for the crossing," the Doe suggested.

The Doe positioned the sword in the middle of Knight's back, held in place with shoulder straps. The Knight practiced wide arm movements, then confirmed the placement would suffice. He decided to carry the armor to the river's edge, just in case.

The Duck led the Doe and the Knight upstream. They walked for a long way, crossing the large meadow of fragrant clover. The Knight looked over his shoulder, squinting to see the Castle Road across the river. He slowed his pace.

"We are walking away from the Castle; my travels on the other side of the river will be quite long! Perhaps the Wolves will arrive before we can warn the villagers!"

"It is better to cross where the river has a gentle current than to be swept over the waterfall, never to arrive at the Castle at all," said the Doe.

The Knight remembered the waterfall and certain death. "Perhaps I could practice at the pond again?"

"Time is not our friend. We must continue on our journey," reminded the Doe.

"You have learned quickly and will be able to cross the river!" said the Duck. Both the Doe and the Duck encouraged the Knight as they walked.

The path ended at a small babbling brook. The Duck, the Doe, and the Knight followed the babbling brook to the river. Vibrant green clover sloped gently down to the river's edge, sunlight dancing over the rippling surface. The Knight rested the armor at the base of a tall tree. "The river is much wider and deeper at this spot, but the current is gentle," repeated the Duck. "This is the place to cross. There is a path on the other side that will take you to the Castle Road."

The Knight hesitated at the river's edge, not sure leaving the armor behind was wise. The Knight frowned, uncertain about the new swimming skills. The Doe and the Duck were accomplished swimmers and didn't understand how crossing any distance was overwhelming for a beginner. Perhaps it would be better to stay and fight the Wolves instead; after all, the Knight had slayed the dragon!

The Doe read the doubt on the Knight's face. "You must cross. I cannot convince the Castle to raise defenses; only you can save them."

"This is the place to cross," the Duck repeated, reassuring the Knight. "It is much like the water in the pond, just a bit deeper. You have proven you can do this in practice."

"I would like to practice more!" The Knight's sword felt heavy and cumbersome.

A flock of ducks flew overhead, quacking in concert.

"The Wolves are advancing." The Duck fixed eyes with the Knight. "We must cross now."

The Knight stepped into the water, feeling the pull of the current and cold depth of the water.

"Float like the log," said the Duck.

"Move feet and hands rhythmically, as if running on a path," said the Doe.

Keep my head up and breathe! thought the Knight.

The Knight launched into the dark depths, icy water entering through the nose and stinging the eyes. Sunlight flickered off the top of the water as the Knight surfaced. The current carried the Knight downstream more quickly than expected.

"Stay calm, and continue to move your hands and feet. Aim for the fallen tree on the other side," coached the Duck.

The Knight could see a large tree that had fallen into the river. It was downstream; the duck was using the current to their advantage.

"Focus on the tree, this is where we can climb out of the river." The Doe was swimming just behind the Knight, watching the tree as she swam. "Focus on the tree."

At the halfway point, the Knight felt the weight of the sword even more keenly and was panting. The taste of water, usually refreshing, was a warning to keep the head up. The Knight heard the Duck from ahead call, "You are more than halfway! You are swimming well! Keep kicking your feet to move forward!"

"We can do this together; the tree is in reach!"

It wasn't really in reach, thought the Knight, but turning back was now a longer swim than continuing forward. "Focus on the tree" was the mantra.

The Duck reached the bank first, hopping up next to the tree. "You are very close! You can make it to the tree!" The Duck paused, calculating the current and the approach the Knight was taking. "Now that you are closer, aim for where I am standing on the tree!"

The Duck positioned herself on top of the massive tree, about a third of the way into the water.

The Doe moved up closer, as she could hear the Knight's labored breathing. She spoke calmly and with confidence. "This crossing is challenging for both of us. The Duck has shown us the way, now we must follow her to the tree. There we can climb out and rest."

The Knight was renewed in spirit, albeit nearly exhausted physically. "Focus on the tree. There we can rest" was the augmented mantra. The Knight looked forward to a rest!

"Float to the tree," the Duck instructed. The Knight was happy to comply, floating into the embrace of the fallen tree's limbs. With arms wrapped around a sturdy branch, the Knight paused to breathe. The Doe climbed the bank near the base of the tree, clearly fatigued, gazing across to their starting point across the great river.

"Look how far we've come! This was truly a great swim!"

The Knight celebrated quietly, taking stock of the journey and the accomplishment. Climbing along the tree to the bank, the Knight thanked the Duck and the Doe for their guidance.

"We may rest for just a moment," said the Duck. "The Wolves are advancing."

The Duck's flock had continued reconnaissance, reporting on the Wolves' progress as they flew overhead.

"The path is well marked through the forest, intersecting with the Castle Road. We must hurry." The Doe started forward, leading the Knight into the safety of the forest. The Duck returned to her flock, with many thanks and promises to meet again.

The Knight appreciated the company of the Doe through the forest. They discussed the behaviors of the Wolves, as the Doe had seen their ravenous work in other villages.

"The Wolves will not stop until all are defeated," she warned.

Fear and urgency were palpable as she related her stories. The Knight learned all there was to learn from the Doe, noting how the Castle could be used to their advantage with the villagers' help.

The Doe stopped at the edge of the forest. "I must leave you here," she said. "It is not safe for me along the Castle Road."

The Knight embraced the Doe, bid farewell, and ran down the Castle Road ahead of the Wolves.

"I will find you later, and tell you of our brilliant success!" yelled the Knight. "I will be watching," said the Doe.

The Knight knew the Doe would always be a confidant, coach, and ever-present voice.

The Knight used the strategies and knowledge shared by the Doe and the Duck to lead the villagers against the approaching threat, the Wolves. The Doe was right, the villagers were reluctant to believe a ravenous pack would attack their home, as solitary dragons in distant lands had been the only predators they had known. The Knight was trusted and convincing, using experiences and encouragement like the Doe and Duck had used. The villagers worked together to save the Castle, leveraging their strengths and experiences with a shared goal to defeat the Wolves and survive. All lived happily ever after.

Decoding the Parable

Let's explore the parable with the CLEAR Change Method. As we read in the last sentence, our hero realized the strategic goal to protect the Castle and defeat the Wolves. The journey was critical to achieving the ultimate success.

Contrast—define the change to be realized, articulate the value of the change (From This, To That, and Why)

- To save the Village from the Wolves, the Knight had to get across the river—but didn't know how to swim.
- In addition, the Knight had to get across the raging river rapidly. The first idea was to build a bridge (long duration, lots of resources), but because of the

fast-moving Wolves, the Knight had to choose a faster strategy and become a swimmer (urgent timeline, sole accountability).

Leadership—engage formal and informal leaders, understanding interest, influence, and impact

- The Doe is the Knight's leader, sharing her knowledge and experiences about the Wolves, which are her area of expertise. The Doe demonstrates an interest in the Knight's capabilities and ultimate success. In addition, the Doe has a network of expert resources to further develop the Knight. The Doe serves as a mentor and coach.
- The Fish is an expert in swimming, but cannot translate his expertise to the Knight. This informal leader has expertise but not influence on the situation, demonstrating little interest in the Knight. The Doe retains the relationship with the Fish, but hurries on to a more appropriate expert: the Duck.
- The Duck is an expert in swimming, with relatable examples that help teach the Knight. She understands how to leverage the river, both in where to cross and how to play to the Knight's advantage. The Duck also leverages her network to keep tabs on the movement of the Wolves. This is an influential and impactful

leader, although an informal one in the Knight's organizational structure.

Experiences—architect experiences to make it easy to do the new thing the right way

- The Knight needs actual experience to swim across the raging river. The practice session in the pond allows the Knight to build capability and confidence with limited risk. Practicing new skills in a safe environment accelerates development for individuals and teams!
- The Doe knows the Knight must shed the armor, representative of the old process/ constraints of the battles the Knight is used to fighting. She approaches the topic at the pond, as part of the practice session. She and the Duck build on the experiences in the pond to reinforce that the Knight must leave the old way, the armor, behind. They recognize and respect the Knight's expertise in battle as they help figure out how to keep the sword and still swim effectively.
- The Doe and the Duck cross the river with the Knight, creating a team approach to the challenge and leveraging the capabilities of each player for overall success.
- The Doe shares her first-hand experiences about the Wolves with the Knight as they travel together through

the forest to the Castle road. This knowledge-sharing experience prepares the Knight for the battle ahead, building the Knight's capability to lead the villagers with confidence.

Accountability—establish clear roles and ownership for the planned elements and outcomes

- The Knight very much wants the Doe and the Duck to facilitate crossing the river. The Doe is an effective leader, refusing to take on the burden to carry the Knight. She has provided coaching and resources to enable the Knight to do so independently. If the Knight relies completely on her to do the heavy lifting, they will *both* go over the waterfall and fail to accomplish their goal. There is no question: the Knight is accountable for crossing the river.
- The Duck is clearly accountable for navigating the river and demonstrates expertise both in the pond and during the crossing to clarify the goal (the tree) and leverage conditions (the current) to make the crossing easier for the Knight.
- The Knight is accountable for communicating the threat of the Wolves to the Village and the Castle. By the end of the story, the Knight steps into this role confidently.

Reinforcement—reinforce the desired outcomes and celebrate interim successes, driving to the finish line

- The Doe and the Duck are masters of reinforcement, defining interim successes for the Knight (practice goals in the pond, recalling the relatable examples used to teach, coaching during the crossing and at key milestones, and the visible target of the Duck on the tree).
- The Doe establishes a focus and a mantra to keep the Knight on task during the crossing (focus on the tree, there we can rest). She repeats the mantra several times as the challenge and fatigue set in, refreshing the phrase at the halfway point to further reinforce the value of completing the challenge. The Doe marks the milestones based on her own fatigue and accomplishment alongside the Knight, creating and reinforcing the culture of the team. Using a simple mantra or rallying cry for a challenge is effective in reinforcing the goal and ensuring the team is progressing together.
- As the Knight is learning how to swim and meeting the interim challenge of crossing the river, it could be easy to forget the reason they need to accomplish this goal in the first place, to defeat the Wolves. The Doe and the Duck remind the Knight at key points that the Wolves are advancing, keeping the bigger picture in

mind as they address interim challenges.

- As the Knight progresses through each stage of the journey, the Duck and the Doe leave an imprint, reinforcing their support and encouragement with plans to meet again. The Knight replicates this approach with the villagers far after they have departed.

Discussion Questions

- Why does the Doe help the Knight?
- How does the Doe convince the Knight to change?
- What is different about the Fish vs the Duck?
- How does the Duck show leadership?
- When is the Knight resistant to change? How does it resolve?
- How did the Doe establish a deliberate journey for effective change?

Discussion Questions (with Answers)

- Why does the Doe help the Knight?

The Doe is a caring leader who has experienced the destruction of the Wolves—she does not want to see the Knight / the Village to suffer the same fate. The Doe is committed to helping others succeed.

- How does the Doe convince the Knight to change?

The Doe shares her personal experiences with the Wolves to create a picture of the future if the Knight does not change. She references the impending threat continually, reinforcing the urgency for change. She helps the Knight progress, learn new skills, and understand how the environment has changed. She especially encourages through the challenging times, when the Knight would like to turn back. The Doe understands what motivates the Knight—protecting others—and she leverages those beliefs to encourage action, resulting in new capabilities (personal change) in learning how to swim, and shares her knowledge to save the Village from Wolves (environmental change—predators attacking the Village rather then sending the Knight to vanquish a solitary dragon).

- What is different about the Fish vs the Duck?

Both the Fish and the Duck are expert swimmers. The Fish, however, cannot relate to or coach those who have different innate abilities. The Duck, on the other hand, can translate expertise in terms and actions the Knight can understand and apply.

- How does the Duck show leadership?

The Duck leads through example by swimming the raging river with the Knight, providing relatable coaching and inspiration throughout. She sets interim goals for the Knight, communicating often with progress updates and encouragement. In addition, the Duck uses her resources (the other Ducks) to gain new insights on the situation, again communicating for the Knight's benefit and support. I'd love to have a leader like the Duck!

- When is the Knight resistant to change? How does it resolve?

The Knight's resistance is best represented by the armor that must be left behind. The armor is the "old ways," a barrier to progress in the new ways of swimming. The armor only slows the Knight down. Keeping it on means failing at the goal of crossing the river. The Knight is hesitant, holding the armor close until the very last moment; the Knight must trust the Doe and the Duck and remove the armor to survive.

- How did the Doe establish a deliberate journey for effective change?

The Doe communicated the urgent issue of the Wolves, engaged her resources (the Fish and the Duck), developed the Knight through experiences, held the Knight accountable while modeling accountability herself, and reinforced the case for change at key milestones along the journey. The Doe served as strategist, leader, mentor, and teammate for the Knight's ultimate success.

Application Questions

- What is the equivalent of the Wolves for your business?
- Where are the situations where you want to build bridges (a safe solution that is eventually effective, but nonoptimal) when you really need to learn to swim (riskier, innovative, and more effective solution)? Where do you need to innovate?
- Who are the experts in your organization? Who are the Fish? Who are the Ducks? How do you know?
- What is the cadence and value of reinforcement? Who are the leaders who do this well? Who does not know how to do this?
- What are the intermediate focus points on your strategic journey? Are they well known? Does your organization have a common mantra?
- What biases inhibit you or your organization? Did you assign a gender to the Knight through a bias? Did anyone think the Doe and the Duck were overreacting about the Wolves because they were female? Or not

credible leaders / experts because they were female? Who in your organization is hindered due to unconscious bias?

- What experiences could you architect to better forward your strategy and change agenda? And who can lead?

PARABLE 2

The NewBees

Once upon a time, on a farm in the middle of nowhere, there was a productive beehive. Farmer Eller had installed a clean white box hive at the edge of his pasture just beyond the barn. The EllerBees, named after the Farmer, grew in number readily, reaping the benefit of the Farmer's pastures and fields. All were content and productive.

In the third spring of the EllerBee colony, the number of bees began to overgrow the hive. The nearby fields, once fragrant and plentiful, were not enough to sustain the hive. As a result, the production of the hive was decreasing at a rapid rate—the population would not survive another season.

They sent a group of scouts out to explore beyond the fields, searching for new routes and additional sources of nourishment. The campaigns were challenging, as the pasture was sparse and no meadows were identified within the standard flight radius.

A selected scout squadron was dispatched to push the boundaries, as times were desperate. The EllerBee squadron flew to the edge of the flight radius to the south, deemed to be the most probable location of fresh meadows. The Squadron smelled fresh water to the southeast, with hints of floral fragrance they could only imagine was a fresh meadow of a considerable size. The Squadron readied for the extraordinarily long flight, recognizing the point of no return was close at hand.

"The future of the EllerBees depends on us!" they buzzed, flying as directly as possible to the growing fragrance and sound of water. "There!" they cried in unison, as bees do. "We have found it!"

Indeed, the Squadron had found a vast field of clover and wildflowers, bountiful and untouched. The smell of rushing water, emanating from a vibrant, babbling brook, added to the intoxicating fragrance. The Squadron was ecstatic, buzzing in circles, landing on flowers, soaking in nectar. They were gleeful, triumphant...and exhausted.

"We must return and tell the others! This is a great triumph!" some of the EllerBee squadron said.

"How shall we return without rest?" others cried in protest. "And how shall we convince the others to come here? It is too far!"

The insurmountable challenge of reaching the Clover Meadow invalidated the accomplishment of discovering fresh resources.

"We are an elite Squadron, young and fearless—and we are at the end of our range. There is no way to guide the mainstream Workers to this location successfully."

The Squadron had to think very hard about how to make the journey accessible and successful for their hive.

As the Squadron flew home, they identified key stopping points along the journey. They used their fatigue to gauge distance between stops, with more frequent stops within the expanse of the Clover Meadow, as this would be the end of the journey. They scouted broad sections of thick foliage, marking tree or rock formations as good areas for rest. The path was not the most direct; they flew close to the perimeter of the nearby woods, as they needed to avoid the mid-summer heat. With finely tuned navigation and memory, the Squadron mapped their journey to the Clover Meadow and the bounty it provided.

Late into the night, the Squadron finally returned to the EllerBee Colony. The overcrowded hive forced the Squadron to swarm on a rafter outside the barn. Swarms outside the hive had become a regular occurrence.

"The food supply we located is too far for the EllerBee Workers. We need to find a different location. We need to find food for the hive," said the Squadron leader.

"Perhaps we need our own hive," said one of the younger scouts.

"After all, we are forced to swarm in uncomfortable and exposed surroundings," buzzed another.

"I can still smell the sweet fragrance of the Clover Meadow," observed another.

The Squadron quickly decided the only course of action to address the food shortage for the EllerBee hive was to propose an innovative solution: to form a new sub-colony adjacent to the Clover Meadow. A breakaway faction would result in a new productive colony, reducing the burden on the EllerBee hive. The Squadron decided to present this option to the EllerBee Queen the next day.

"We have found a bountiful field of fragrant clover," the Squadron reported to the EllerBee Queen.

"Excellent work! I knew I had chosen the right team!" The EllerBee Queen was satisfied, ready to move on to the next order of business.

"Unfortunately, the Clover Meadow is well beyond the standard flight radius. It was difficult for our Squadron to make the journey and return; we fear it is not a usable option for our hive," the Squadron continued. "We have another option. We propose we populate a new colony in the Clover Meadow. This would reduce demand on the flora in the current flight radius and reduce the overcrowding in our current hive. There would be more space for the EllerBee Colony to produce and grow. There would be more resources to go around, and the EllerBee Workers wouldn't have to fly impossible distances every day."

"Why would you want to leave the comfort of our fine hive here at EllerBee?" asked the EllerBee Queen.

She understood the need for fresh fields. She felt the overwhelming pressure for space outside her chamber. She knew the restlessness of the younger population would continue to grow under these conditions. The EllerBee Queen had little control over the condition of the hive; that was the domain of the Farmer. The risk of flight beyond the safe radius, long determined in the hive's history, was not appealing to her traditional upbringing. The bravery to concoct and propose such a radical break was ridiculous—but it was also Remarkable. Inspirational. Visionary.

"I do not understand how you will succeed," the Queen said. "But I am willing to allow you to try." The Squadron gasped, then buzzed in excitement. "You must have a Queen to survive," the Queen continued. "I will not require any of the Princess Bees to go with you, but if you can convince one of them to fly with you, I will allow it. Similarly, only volunteers may go with you—there cannot be any coercion or pressure to embark on such a risky journey."

For the NewBees, as they now called themselves, this was a victory!

Armed with the story of beautiful Clover Meadow, the sanctioning of the EllerBee Queen, and an aggressive timeline, the NewBees convinced the eldest Princess to embark on the adventure. The Squadron was well connected and recruited the finest collection of Workers for the NewBee hive. The Squadron planned the move carefully, sending sortie missions to scout the location of the new hive.

The Squadron tested the route to the Clover Meadow, complete with rest stops, inviting Workers to join the NewBees based on their strength and building experience. With a few adjustments, they established an accessible and repeatable route.

With a defined flight path, the next step was clear: establish the NewBee hive.

The NewBee advance team selected a grove of tall sycamore trees as the best location for the hive. Located at the edge of the forest bordering the meadow, the trees stood on a bluff overlooking a babbling brook. The breezes from the brook danced in the large leaves, embracing the sweet fragrance of the clover among the branches.

The NewBees searched tirelessly among the boughs for the perfect spot. In the crook of one of the larger trees, several feet above the ground, they spied an irregularity in the craggy bark. A small crevice in the bark was scarred over and hidden in the protection of the surrounding boughs. With a bit of perseverance, the NewBees peeled away enough bark to discover a large hollow cavity in the tree, formed by interrupted growth and some years of decay. The space was long and moderately wide, but the walls were irregular and convoluted—very different from the straight walls of the EllerBee hive. The NewBees were inspired. The rippled tree walls weren't what they were used to, but they were ideal for anchoring layers of honeycomb.

Materials were plentiful, challenges were met with enthusiasm, and the NewBee Squadron and Workers learned from each other as they constructed the initial framework with energy and anticipation. Pride of ownership grew as the hive progressed. This was their NewBee home!

On moving day, the NewBee Squadron prepared the newly named NewBee Queen and her troops for the flight ahead.

"It is a long flight, well beyond the EllerBee flight radius," the NewBees told the crowd. "We have positioned mileposts along the way for rest, refreshment, and for some of you, the opportunity to return to the EllerBee hive. The decision to move is yours to make—and a journey you must take on your own. The NewBee Squadron knows the way, and will provide encouragement, advice, and support. You may travel at your own pace. Our shared goal is to establish the NewBee hive in the Clover Meadow, where nectar is sweet and the hive is able to grow."

With that, select members of the Squadron surrounded the NewBee Queen and escorted her to the first rest stop.

"The crowd is enormous!" the NewBee Queen observed. "Are we sure we all will fit in the NewBee hive?"

"We've only just begun," said the Squadron.

They continued on with cautious optimism.

The crowd thinned along the route. A reasonable band of Workers was already queued at the last rest stop within the EllerBee flight radius. The Squadron again addressed the crowd.

"Here is our point of no return. If we progress beyond this stop, we cannot return; our journey must then continue to a new hive. We will not all make the journey successfully; for those who do, the Clover Meadow will provide new vitality and productivity for all."

A loud buzz resonated from the remaining crowd, and most continued on; some, however, turned back toward the EllerBee home without shame or regret.

When they finally arrived at the Clover Meadow, the NewBee Queen viewed the hive with mixed emotions. First, she felt excitement—it was hers! This was a rare opportunity to lead and grow a new community. The inside of a hollow tree, however, was a far cry from the orderly construct of the manufactured hive box, and the construction was still in progress.

As she settled into her chamber, the Squadron reviewed the construction plan and reassured the young queen of the bounty their new home would provide. She had smelled the sweet fragrance as they had flown over the Clover Meadow, and the strange yet comforting coolness of the air from the babbling brook nearby.

"We are home, my Queen," said the Squadron, helping her get comfortable with her new surroundings, regaling her as the Queen of the NewBee hive. She was a bit nervous, but tried to stay calm. Only time would tell of their success...or ultimate failure.

The NewBees had built their hive with only a small portion of the original swarm having the strength to make it to the colony. Workers progressed in their tasks, learning new skills and new responsibilities from the NewBee Workers who had constructed the initial framework. Some Workers could not adjust to the new environment and departed. Regular reviews with the Squadron kept the progress moving forward, sometimes at the expected pace and sometimes slower. The colony grew strong and adapted to the challenges of a natural hive, feasted on the abundance of nourishment, and established a thriving hive structure that hummed with productivity.

By the end of the season, they had a well-functioning NewBee hive, with a responsive, productive and growing colony. The NewBee Queen was well satisfied, and all was well.

This could be the end of the story...but there is more to tell.

Back at the EllerBee colony, the Farmer checked in on his hive. Last time he checked on it closely, he had noticed it was overpopulated, and was considering getting a second hive. Farmer Eller made a fair bit of income from the hive's products—honey, some beeswax, pollination services on rare occasions—but despite the overpopulation in spring, there was a reduction in productivity this season.

On this visit, the Farmer was surprised to see the hive had lost a substantial population of bees. How could this have happened? Was there a plague? A storm? The colony seemed vibrant, production was moving at its normal pace, and the EllerBee Queen was healthy. The colony's drop in population was a mystery.

That afternoon, the Farmer overheard his Neighbor Farmer to the south bragging about the hive he had discovered in an unused corner of his farm this season. The bees were strong and swift; he planned to use this colony to facilitate the pollination in the coming year. Other Farmers in the region were complaining about crop challenges, to the point that it could possibly impact next season's plantings; they, too, were considering bee-keeping on the property but didn't have the knowledge or a source for healthy bees. (Author's Note: OK, I may not have depicted the reality of modern farming, but remember, this is a parable!) The Farmer decided to observe his hive, as the mystery remained of interest to him.

The Farmer tracked a swarm of his bees to the outer limits of the property, near the fallow field of his Neighbor Farmer (who had been bragging). The bees seemed to fly up to an imaginary wall, hover, and turn back. Now and again, a rogue bee would fly on into the next field, sometimes returning quickly—and sometimes not returning at all. The Farmer knew this was very odd, as bees always return to the hive. It is in their nature. They are colony based and cannot survive alone. There must be an explanation.

On the third day, the Farmer tracked one of the rogue bees from his property to a grove of sycamore trees. Although hidden among the branches, the Farmer could see where the NewBee hive was located. The NewBee Workers were well organized, functional and productive; the Farmer imagined a hive dripping with honey.

He suspected right away that these were a faction of his EllerBees. He did not know how they managed to break away and form a new hive, and he didn't care. He knew they belonged with him, on his farm, in his colony. After all, he had paid for these bees. Living on their own in the Clover Meadow was a waste of his money!

The Farmer left them, for now. With an established NewBee Queen, he could not simply return the colony to the existing hive. He would have to build a new hive box and allow the colony to continue apart from the original hive—which they would be permitted to do, but only within his boundaries (and with a clear return on his investment).

The Farmer met with the Neighbor Farmer and negotiated relocation of the hive at the end of the season. The Farmer wanted to share the benefit of the new hive's pollination habits, but within his control and ownership. He established a value proposition, and could now charge for hive rental and pollination services across the region.

The NewBees had no idea. The hive was humming and highly productive. Many of the NewBees were stronger and more vital than they had been in the past. The NewBee Queen was radiant, the population was booming. There were known concerns: not all the Workers were well positioned in the organic structure of the hive, preferring the traditional-hive shape and channels; the Squadron was new to leadership, and not every process had been standardized; assessments were regular, but progress varied; and the impact of the water droplets from the babbling brook could affect the flight of inexperienced bees. Despite these setbacks, however, the progress was overall remarkable. The hive was healthy, and there was an overall sense of success and pride in constructing something anew.

One morning, the NewBee Queen awoke to the smell of something she could not quite place...a distant fragrance memory that repulsed her. It was only too late that she realized it was smoke.

The cough and buzz of the Squadron surrounded her as the Farmer's glove plucked her from her chamber. Darkness surrounded her. The buzz seemed to retreat, then follow at a constant hum in the distance.

The Farmer placed the NewBee Queen in the new, manufactured hive at the edge of his property, within flying distance of the Clover Meadow. The Squadron, committed to protecting her, swarmed the hive and guided her into the new chamber. She was safe, albeit confused. The structure of the new hive felt familiar, yet uninviting and cold. The Queen and the NewBees had grown used to the imperfections of the hollow tree and the flexibility it provided for all the colony inhabitants.

The colony they had built was left behind—the Farmer destroyed the hollow tree hive to protect his investment. Only a few of the NewBee Workers lived to follow their queen.

The colony slowly rebuilt itself by leveraging the lessons of the hollow tree experience. The NewBee colony survived, but never achieved the same productivity they had achieved in the Clover Meadow. Those who remembered the hollow tree experience longed for the freedom and responsibility the challenging adventure had provided.

A few seasons later, a plague descended on the bee populations of the area. In just a few days, the entire population of local hives was eradicated, leaving few Workers and even fewer Queens in its wake. Every hive would require repopulation with a new Queen, except one: the NewBee hive.

Many postulated the hollow tree experience of the NewBees ensured the strength and resilience of the colony. The NewBees became the foundational colony of Queens and bees that repopulated the region, ensuring economic and agricultural viability for years to come.

Decoding the Parable

Let's explore the parable with the CLEAR Change Method. The NewBees realized the original strategic goal to protect the hive, although not directly through their idea to create an independent colony. The experiment failed because the NewBees did not fully understand the leadership model or true decision-maker—in other words, they didn't think about how the Farmer could destroy their hive and move them back to the farm. However, the bold idea of striking out paid off in the long term, with greater resilience for those who had taken the risk to experience a new environment and taken on a challenge with innovative thinking.

Contrast—define the change to be realized, show the value of the change (From This, To That, and Why)

- The overburdened colony/hive was running out of resources and space; it was essential to expand into new space in order to survive.
- Production was declining because of limited resources and space. Expansion was necessary to maintain output (from the Farmer's perspective).

Leadership—engage formal and informal leaders, understanding interest, influence, and impact

- Bee colonies have a clearly defined hierarchy. With a bit of literary license (and forgiveness from my bee-keeping friends), the parable establishes these roles:
  - Queen—the leader of the colony. There is only one Queen for each hive
  - Squadron—the collective of next-level bees who serve the Queen
  - Workers—the collective of those who build the hive and do the work to keep the operation running
- In the EllerBee colony, the Squadron took on an informal leadership role as scouts, experts who would explore the area for new resources. These bees later became the informal leaders in the NewBee colony, sharing their expertise with an inexperienced Queen leader.
- The EllerBee Queen was the head of the hive and its operations, but her leadership influence did not extend beyond the walls of the hive. As she stated to herself, creating a new hive was the Farmer's domain, and the NewBees didn't take his role into account or have the global experience of Farm operations. Inexperience with the larger picture can blind you, especially if leadership is not forthcoming with critical information. If the Ellerbee Queen had warned the NewBees

about the Farmer, they may have approached the issue differently.

Experiences—architect experiences to make it easy to do the new thing the right way

- The journey beyond the traditional flight radius was a challenge only the strongest Squadron could undertake. Assigning unique challenges to highly talented team members is a great learning experience for both leaders and those who take on the journey.
    - The Squadron consistently acted as one team, deliberating options and inputs from each member, but speaking with one voice in decisions and accomplishments. This teamwork is key to their strengths and capabilities.
- The Squadron recruited the Queen and Workers for the new colony; they created a mission, described the new home based on their own experiences, and allowed independent decision-making. This ensured they had support, even as the crowd of volunteers waned during the journey. Those who remained bought into the purpose, the innovative environment, the new colony and all the challenges it presented. These shared Experiences likely helped them through their difficulties.

- The Squadron prepared the NewBee hive in anticipation of the relocation journey, making it easier for the NewBee Queen and others to acclimate, adapt, and produce. The name of "NewBee" and the "welcome home mentality" were key to establishing the new normal.
- The Squadron kept their word that they would not shame or criticize any who did not make the journey or who turned back. Any negative or derisive comments against those who chose not to come would have dismantled the purpose-driven culture of acceptance in the NewBee colony. This purpose-driven culture was essential for teamwork through the difficulties in building a new hive, which was critical for their survival.
- The hollow tree presented new challenges to a colony that had only known the order of a manufactured hive. The unpredictable nature of a new environment coupled with a lack of experience in a new or innovative environment was difficult; some thrived, and some did not do well (and departed). Only through the experience of the NewBee colony did learning take place.
- The Farmer learned about the NewBees' success from observation. He later positioned the NewBee hive on his property within flying distance of the Clover

Meadow. In this way, he reaped the benefit of expanded resources, a wider flight radius, and additional service contracts with the neighbors without sacrificing ownership rights.

Accountability—establish clear roles and ownership for the planned elements and outcomes

- The EllerBee Queen sets expectations that any bee could relocate but only on their own decision. There should be no pressure applied to go and no shame ascribed to those who chose not to go.
- The Squadron established clear decision rights on each bee to choose to continue or return home at the outset of the journey and at the point of no return.
- The roles within the colony were clearly defined (by bee culture), with known responsibilities and hierarchy.
- As discussed, the EllerBee Queen did not actually have the decision rights to approve the NewBee colony proposal, but she "allowed it" to move forward anyway. She didn't warn the NewBees about the Farmer. The NewBee colony, especially the NewBee Queen, had to be upset when they were moved back to the Farm without recourse or discussion.
- The Farmer reinforced his supreme authority by mov-

ing the NewBee colony to the new hive on his Farm. Property lines govern ownership of any product or service resulting from the bees' work, resulting in cash flow for the Farm. Had they understood this, the NewBees could have weighed the risk and uncertainty of breaking away vs the security of the Farmer's care.

Reinforcement—reinforce the desired outcomes and celebrate interim successes, drive to the finish line

- The Squadron coached the NewBee Queen during the journey, celebrating the rest stops as milestones and reminding her how important her role was in establishing the new colony—she was the VI...Bee, and was being escorted to ensure her safety and success.
- The Squadron used imagery and fragrance to communicate the value of the new location, even though the journey would be difficult. The destination of Clover Meadow reinforced the bounty and beauty of the new colony, waiting for them at the end of the journey.
- The assessment of productivity and population was a key indicator of health, and the hive to action (standard processes, feedback to Workers, departure of those who could not adapt) to sustain or improve the overall health of the hive and colony.

Discussion Questions

- Which stakeholder did the NewBee Squadron *believe* had authority to approve the new colony? Who *actually* had the authority?
- How would you characterize the EllerBee Queen—engaged? Neutral? Passive aggressive?
- How would you characterize the NewBee Queen? How did she change during the journey?
- How do you think the NewBee colony felt after they established the hollow tree hive? How about when they were moved back to the Farm?
- How did the NewBee leaders establish a deliberate journey for effective change?

Discussion Questions (with Answers)

- Which stakeholder did the NewBee Squadron *believe* had authority to approve the new colony? Who *actually* had the authority?

The NewBee Squadron believed the EllerBee Queen had full authority. In fact, the Farmer was the ultimate authority. The NewBee Squadron did not recognize his level of influence (or even his existence). Missing or not fully appreciating the influence of a stakeholder is a common failure point in change initiatives.

- How would you characterize the EllerBee Queen—engaged? Neutral? Passive aggressive?

Passive-aggressive. The EllerBee Queen does not openly share what she knows, allowing the NewBees to take on more risk than they recognize. She is skeptical, perhaps even sure the NewBees will fail—yet she does not raise any concerns.

- How would you characterize the NewBee Queen? How did she change during the journey?

The NewBee Queen is naïve, taking on responsibility for a large organization early in her career. She learns quickly, mentored by the Squadron and the expert Workers who made the journey, and before long she is running a successful colony.

- How do you think the NewBee colony felt after they established the hollow tree hive? How about when they were moved back to the Farm?

The construction of a new hive in a far-off location under challenging conditions—any NewBee should be proud of the accomplishment! Upon relocation, they lost the exhilaration of the unknown, and perhaps mourned. In addition, the realization of the Farmer's power over the colony would be disheartening and perhaps oppressive. The risks of the new location were mitigated, but their freedom was stripped from them.

- How did the NewBee leaders establish a deliberate journey for effective change?

The Squadron presented the mission to break away and form a new hive as a matter of survival and productivity, with the arduous journey well communicated with knowledge of risk and reward. The physical journey included clear Leadership roles, with respect for the influence yet lack of knowledge with the NewBee Queen. Role accountability was clear (as it is with bees) at the hive, with reinforcement at key milestones on the journey, during construction, and finally through productivity measures.

Application Questions

- Who are the Squadron of informal leaders in your business? Are they allowed to explore their innovative ideas? Are they supported in their proposals? Are they informed of potential risks?
- Who are the localized leaders who reach beyond their remit? Who are the localized leaders who are passive / indifferent, perhaps withholding key information?

- As you consider change, have you established the impact on customers or operations that follow your team's process? Have you engaged the leadership of these downstream operations? Similarly, what do you need from processes and leaders that supply your organization's work?
- How do you help your next generation of talent (the NewBee Queen, the Squadron) understand the broader context of business? How are you mentoring them through specific experiences?
- When an experiment or innovative process fails, how do you respond? How do you identify and apply lessons from the experience? How might you celebrate?
- What biases prevented the bees from predicting the Farmer's actions? How does bias blind you from seeing key influencers or the whole picture of your business?

PARABLE 3

The Warren

Once upon a time, there lived a happy Warren of rabbits. They were excellent builders and had developed a comfortable yet growing community alongside a babbling brook that flowed into a wide river beyond the forest. The main entrance was nestled beneath a giant sycamore tree on the bluff. The Clover Meadow was safe and sunny, thick with white blossoms and sweet perfume.

Early in the spring, the Bunny Communication System (BCS) reported on Farmers who had established fields in the valley beyond the Clover Meadow. The Farmers were rapidly growing their operations. The food chain was disrupted, and many predators were exploring new hunting grounds—including terrifying Wolves. The rabbit community was on high alert, with several warrens already suffering large losses. It was only a matter of time before the wave of predators reached the Clover Meadow.

"We must find a way to protect ourselves," stated Randall. He had served as the Council leader for several years. He was disturbed by the news reports, but skeptical; a wave of predators roaming through the valley was beyond belief.

"We are safe here, in the Clover Meadow," Randall said. "The great tree can help us hide."

The Council members nodded. It was unclear *how* the great sycamore tree could help them hide, but they had learned to just nod when Randall spoke to keep the mood calm and open for discussion. Randall had a reputation for being extremely strict in his interpretation of the Warren laws, with powerful support from the elders and influential Council members.

The Council could not keep the news secret. Stories of destruction and loss spread through the Warren.

"There is no way to protect ourselves against this kind of threat!"

"How will we protect our children, our elders?"

"What will become of us?"

The Warren was chaotic. The Council members had no answers. They needed a way forward, but they were stuck. Randall did the only thing he knew to do—he engaged the community.

"I call upon our best builders, our brightest architects to bring forth ideas. How might we address this new threat and protect our community?" Randall asked.

Eva, one of the brightest builders of the community, heard the call—but had no answers. She had no experience with designing warrens for this level of protection. Eva returned to the banks of the babbling brook to think, hoping to become inspired.

As she watched the water, she saw a Beaver building a lodge near the bank. It was nearly completed, and floated in a natural cove of the brook. While she watched, the Beaver placed a line of branches near the opening of the eddy, not connected to the lodge, but at some distance away. The Beaver swam over to where Eva perched. He was curious why she was watching him so intently.

"Hello, Mr. Beaver. I'm a builder for my Warren. I'm curious—what are you building out there in the brook?" Eva asked, always polite. As a rule, rabbits are very polite and don't talk with other woodland creatures for fear of an altercation. Eva needed help, and she could see the Beaver had unique skills.

"I've nearly finished my family's lodge, just there." The Beaver pointed to the mounded bark structure floating in the eddy. "And now, I'm building the dam that will help protect us."

Eva looked perplexed.

"We build our homes on the water to help protect us from predators," the Beaver went on. "If we are safe and dry in our lodge, and the water is deep around us, we know it is more difficult for Wolves to reach us. We build a dam to block the water flow, placing it so the water rises in the area surrounding the lodge. With deeper water, we have more protection. Because we make it difficult for the predator to reach us, they move on to easier targets and any attack is prevented. We are protected by *how* we build our homes."

Eva absorbed the important principles from her new friend. She returned home to discuss what she had learned about protection with her fellow builders. The Warren could not be protected by deep water, but *how* they built the Warren was an idea to consider. They developed plans based on two principles: first, prevent the predators from entering the Warren; and second, improve the probability of escape if the Warren is breached.

The resulting plans were simple but radically different from the standard Warren construct. Eva had a good sense of the Council's perspective; she had studied past debates with her Grandmother who had served as a Council member for many years. She knew this would be a challenging proposal for the traditionalist Council to approve. The builders, however, were supportive, and had helped Eva create the design, review the risks, and craft the implementation plan. The proposal was logical and sound—but the idea was disruptive.

"I've learned from our neighbor, the Beaver," Eva stated as she started her presentation. Gasps erupted from the Council. "I've learned that protection can have many layers," she continued. "This proposal puts forward two layers: First, reduce the threat of the predator entering our Warren. I propose we build a shadow Warren as a decoy. We will make it so complex that the predators will become lost within the maze. Tired and frustrated, the invader will abandon the effort and depart," Eva said. The Council looked at each other in confusion. "Second, if the predator finds the path into our Warren, we must maximize the pathways for our escape. I propose we create an interlocking set of tunnels between our private family burrows to improve our escape routes."

The Council was aghast. Violate the privacy of the family burrows? Preposterous! Unthinkable!

"We must be able to keep family discussions private. I am sure we have a law about this!" one Council member said.

"I'm not convinced the threat of a mythical intruder who can enter our burrow is even real. This is paranoia, not factual news!" cried another. "We cannot disrupt our lives over a rumor."

"Before this 'predator' nonsense, we were discussing overcrowding in the Warren. We need more space to *live* in; we cannot waste valuable real estate on a Decoy Warren!" recounted a third Council member.

A loud and frantic discussion boiled up with no one really listening to each other. The builders looked down at their feet, shirking away from the political fire.

Eva, however, remained confident.

"Our current escape routes work if the invader comes from the path we anticipate. We know how to escape when a Wolf charges across the Clover Meadow. But if this new predator is as destructive as has been reported, we need more options." Eva paused to let the Council reflect on the recent reports. "With our current design, the Warren does not allow for multiple exit paths. Connecting our burrows allows any family multiple paths to escape, regardless of the intrusion point."

"This would *also* allow for any family to enter any other family's burrow without notice!" one Council member observed.

"Neighbors could hear anything we say in our own burrow!" cried another.

"It's loud enough due to overcrowding—I think we are missing the real priority here!" noted another.

Randall allowed Eva to continue with the proposal. After all, she had convinced the Warren's builders—not an easy group to convince—and they were supportive. Randall recognized some of the quieter Council members *were* convinced, even if he was not. Randall did not like conflict, and he despised operating in areas where he was not the expert. The predatory threat under consideration was anecdotal, reported only recently by other communities; the predator had not been thoroughly investigated or analyzed—taking action on an unconfirmed creature was unacceptable. He had no other solutions; for the wellbeing of the community, he had to support the proposal, even if he didn't believe it would work.

He needed to buy some time to verify the threat and develop more acceptable solutions.

In the midst of the debate, the Bunny Communication System issued an urgent report. The ancestral Warren, located near the edge of the valley, had been consumed. The predatory pack was unidentified, but whatever it was, it was small enough to crawl into the warren's entrance and raid the family burrows! This was unbelievable!

The Warren understood the hunting patterns of Wolves, chasing prey across the fields with great strength and agility. They understood the precision of the Eagles, swooping down from above with extraordinary vision. But an invader in their own homes? This was unfathomable.

They had no time to waste. They needed a solution, and didn't have any better offers. With a quick nod from Randall, the Council approved the proposal, charging the builders to move forward with the plans. They appointed Eva as the project leader.

Construction on the Decoy Warren started early the next day. The design included a complex maze of tunnels, each path doubling back toward the bank of the babbling brook. With any luck, the intruder would become disoriented and fall into the brook. The builders had to work quickly, as news of the attacks had continued through the night. Experienced builders helped the inexperienced builders understand the complex plans. These junior builders were assigned to execute the more standard elements of the plan. The most experienced worked on more challenging tunnels that carried a larger risk of cave-in. Progress was swift and efficient at the start, and Day 1 went according to plan.

"I'd like to recognize Eva for her strong leadership," Randall stated at the daily all-Warren meeting. "We are seeing great progress on this revolutionary plan. We have every confidence this will protect us from the alleged threat experienced by other rabbit communities across our region."

Eva appreciated the public support for the project but felt the threat was real, not "alleged"; perhaps Randall was trying to instill optimism, she rationalized.

On Day 2, Eva returned to the decoy warren worksite to find the junior builders hard at work—but none of the experienced builders were in sight.

"Some Council member asked them to work on some other project," accounted the juniors as they toiled. "They did not say where they were going."

Eva found the experienced builders constructing a new branch of burrows to the existing Warren, located to the east of the main entrance. This area was not included in her plan. She found out that Randall had approved this expansion project prior to the predator crisis, and one of the Council members had reassigned the builders.

Eva returned to the work site quietly, aggravated by the distraction of the expansion project and reassignment of the experienced builders. Her nose twitched in frustration as she watched the junior builders—they were making progress, but their inefficiencies were costing time and perhaps some level of safety as the project progressed. Day 2 was in the books, but not according to plan. Did Randall not realize the protection of the Warren was a priority?

Upon returning to her home burrow that evening, Grandmother sensed Eva's frustrations.

"Tell me about your day on the project, my sweet Lead Builder!" Grandmother teased.

Eva mustered up a small smile. "It was a day all right," she acknowledged.

Eva recounted the day's events to her Grandmother, her tone and anger escalating as she pulled the pieces together.

Eva's Grandmother smiled and caressed Eva's ears.

"It's just the beginning, my love. You've not started the second phase of your plan yet, and *that* is the most contentious." Grandmother shared the elder rabbit chatter regarding the connection of family burrows. "There is strong resistance to this construction, and Randall knows it. He must support you in public but may not support you with the elders or with the Council. Why do you think he pulled your best builders today?"

Eva was shocked and disappointed by her naïve view of today's events. Grandmother had opened her eyes to the possibility that the events of the day were deliberate distractions.

"Randall can only see what he has experienced; he cannot see beyond what has already been. My dear Eva, you must work with Randall, the leader of our Warren. You have the talent to lead us through this crisis, but you have to meet Randall where he is. If you do not, he will undermine your progress and we will all pay the price. Consider how you might make it easy for Randall to do the right thing."

Eva considered the conversation with her Grandmother as the work at the decoy warren progressed. Her builders were all back on the project, having completed the expansion project in record time. The junior builders were learning quickly because of the unique experiences the complicated decoy warren presented. The team moved to seasoning the tunnels, legitimizing the decoy warren with the trappings and smells of a real warren.

Phase One and Day 3 were complete.

Eva met individually with many of the Council members, sharing the updates on the decoy warren progress and listening closely to their reactions. She was listening for support, for concerns, for rumors, for distractions. Over the nine members of the Council, she knew that some were interested and engaged with the new reality and were quite supportive of her team's efforts. A few expressed little interest in her plans or progress, focused instead on the crowding of the Warren. Two remained neutral, perhaps scared, somewhat resistant but open to new ideas.

She learned Randall wanted to be optimistic, but just didn't see the path forward. He was very concerned the elder rabbits would take offense if he supported any change to the private burrows they enjoyed. Randall was in a tough position, and outside of his expertise. Grandmother was right: Eva had to make it easy for him to do the right thing.

Eva scheduled an immersive experience—a listening party—for Randall and the Council members. She arranged for her Grandmother and her elder rabbit friends to meet in one of the new burrows constructed in the expansion; they would chat loudly (as they often did) and the Council members would listen from another burrow to discern what could be heard. Eva was nervous; this demonstration would determine if she had support to move forward or if the plan was in jeopardy. The future wellbeing of the Warren rested on this experience.

No rabbits had moved into the expansion as yet, so the walls were freshly cut—the worst acoustic conditions. Eva took a deep breath, straightened her ears, and yelled as she approached. Eva's voice echoed louder than normally heard in a populated warren.

"Thank you for proving the point that we have a need for privacy in our Warren!" snidely commented one of the more conservative Council members. "Are we done?"

"Not yet, we've only just started," replied Eva. She nodded to her Grandmother, who gathered her elder rabbit friends in the adjacent burrow and started their normal chat-fest. Eva returned to the Council in the larger burrow. "Listen. Can you make out the conversation?" Ears twitched and flexed, straining to hear the details of the conversation.

"I only hear a murmur," said one Council member.

"I think I heard my name," said another, blushing.

"We should inhabit this space immediately. We are so overcrowded!" said another, not really addressing the current topic.

"It's a dull rumble, much like we hear every day in the Warren," stated Randall.

This is a quote I could use, thought Eva.

"Now, let's understand the impact of Phase Two," said Eva.

She hopped to the back of the burrow, removing a leaf to expose a small tunnel with a visible clump of foliage and fur positioned just inside the opening.

"This is an emergency tunnel, constructed between this burrow and the burrow where my Grandmother is chatting with her friends," Eva said. "There is a similar plug at the other end of the tunnel, and I've asked the elders to congregate near this tunnel to maximize our ability to hear them."

Eva led Randall out of the larger burrow, motioning him into the adjacent burrow to observe the position of the chatting elders. Many of the Council members followed, but none said a word.

"As my Grandmother stated, the elders are chatting at normal volume and we positioned them at the opening of the new connection tunnel. We agreed the acoustics under these new construction conditions result in much greater transmission of sound than in our current Warren. And yet, as you kindly observed, the conversation sounds like a dull rumble, much like we hear every day in our Warren. This means that the escape tunnels would not infringe on our privacy at all."

The Council remained silent. Randall twitched his nose. He was impressed, but continued to say nothing.

"I'd now like to demonstrate how the escape tunnel system works, should we need to use it."

Four junior builders appeared next to Eva, while Grandmother and the elder rabbits retired to the main tunnel to watch. The juniors positioned themselves in the center of the burrow and relaxed as if enjoying a rest after a long day of building.

Then, Eva let out an emergency signal (known only to rabbits). The juniors jumped to their haunches; two exited through the main tunnel while the other two leaped into the escape tunnel. The plug disintegrated with the forceful contact, and the two juniors exploded through the other side into the larger burrow where several Council members had remained. They flashed through the next emergency tunnel section, passed the two juniors in the main tunnel, and circled back around to Eva at the start point. The Council members gazed at each other through the ends of the escape tunnel, barely blinking in awe at what they had seen.

"That was spectacular!" whispered Randall. He was excited, yet cautious; he could not afford to be too optimistic as the threat had not been verified.

"I'd like to recognize Eva for her strong leadership," Randall stated. "We are seeing great progress on this revolutionary plan. We have every confidence this will protect us from the alleged threat experienced by other rabbit communities across our region." Once again, he provided the superficial support Eva needed to continue construction. Randall was gaining confidence in the plan, but he kept it to himself.

The feedback from the elders was generally positive, and the demonstration was a success. Eva asked Randall for a quiet word beyond earshot of the others.

"I have the sense you have not been as committed to our success as your words would suggest," Eva said quietly. "I believe you've had doubts on whether we would be successful. You know, if *we* are unsuccessful, *you* are unsuccessful—unless you have another protection project underway?"

Eva pushed the button. She needed to understand if he was being held accountable for the success of the project, or if she was to be the scapegoat should the project—and the Warren—fail to protect itself.

Randall looked at Eva with respect, now speaking privately. "I was not confident you would complete construction or resolve our privacy issues. But I also do not have a sound alternative. We are looking for partners to take us in should our Warren be destroyed. That is my only avenue, if *we* fail."

Randall was sharing it all. He knew he held full accountability for the wellbeing of the Warren. He also knew he had to put his trust in Eva and her team to deliver.

The demonstration on Day 4 concluded with the arrival of refugees from the ancestral Warren, attacked days before. The Warren welcomed the few surviving rabbits with food and shelter. They shared a detailed account of the predators' attack, a harrowing day of devastation and loss. The survivors confirmed how the beasts invaded the Warren through the main tunnel with great agility. The predator was real; they named it the Fox.

Over the next two days, Eva and her team built the escape tunnels, connecting each of the burrows in the Warren to create a flexible set of escape routes. Randall communicated the plans to the Warren, sharing his experiences and his concerns. He genuinely recognized and praised the team's progress, and he asked how he could help resolve issues. Most importantly, he spoke from the heart about the reality of the threat and the promise of the plan.

Randall prepared his remarks for Day 6 with care. Based on the report from the refugees, he needed to create a sense of urgency in the Warren. He needed to instill confidence in Eva's plan. He needed to recognize the possibility that not all would survive. He needed to prepare the Warren for an attack, and the residents needed to know how to respond.

Randall could see the community was anxious and uncertain. Eva suggested a practice drill; practicing the new escape routes before the Fox attacked would build confidence and improve their survival rates. He brought up the idea with selected Council members and they agreed. In addition to preparation, a drill would provide another opportunity for reluctant Council members to see the plan in action.

Early the next morning, Randall stood outside the emergency exit tunnel, assigning the resistant Council members to time how quickly the Warren could exit. He sounded the alarm, waking the Warren from a deep sleep. As expected, an early wave of rabbits emerged from the main exit tunnel.

"This is no improvement. I should have slept in," sneered one dissenting Council member.

"I'm glad I'm not in that crowd," humphed another, checking the timer.

"It's so crowded, there is no way to get out quickly," the other started. "We must expand our—" He stopped mid-sentence, awestruck by the scene before him.

Rabbits were popping out of the ground like wildflowers! Several escape-tunnel openings exploded with the force of rabbits jumping from the tunnel system into the safety of the Clover Meadow. With so many escape hatches, the frenetic scene manifested as a cloud of rabbits, veiling the location of any individual for added protection. The scene was overwhelming and fabulous at the same time.

"We have learned a great deal from this practice drill, and I thank you for your active participation," Randall told the Warren. "We know the threat of predators invading our home is real. Now we know how to respond, and how to protect ourselves and our families. Thank you."

Eva was beaming with pride. Her plan was actually working! She recognized the builders for their tireless efforts, and worked with the team to refit the escape tunnels.

It was a moment of calm in the storm; the Bunny Communication System reported the invasion was close at hand, just a day's journey from the Clover Meadow.

The invasion came in the stillness of early morning. The Foxes emerged from the forest and gathered at the entrance to the decoy warren. The seasoning had worked, drawing the attackers to the decoy entrance. The scratching and howling roused Randall; he sounded the alarm, running through the Warren to wake the community to the threat next door. Quickly, just as they had during the drill, the rabbits began to evacuate.

The plan worked well for the majority of the community. The early rabbits exiting through the escape tunnel were undetected as they were far away from the decoy entrance. Soon, the predators were alerted to the frantic movement by the sound of countless rabbits hopping across the Clover

Meadow. Thanks to the maze, it took the Foxes a long time to reach the surface again.

The elder rabbits were slow to exit and slower to hop—many were unfortunately lost to the predators' appetites. The Council rabbits who doubted the threat were not prepared to escape and were lost at the main exit of the Warren. Agile and decisive parents stewarded children, hiding among the brush and rocks at outposts within the forest or along the banks of the babbling brook. Frustrated and tired, the predator pack moved on to new territories.

The attack could have been devastating. They could have lost everything.

Eva drew in a deep breath, calming her pounding heartbeat. It was still a blow, but not nearly as bad of an attack as it would have been, had the warren been defenseless. Eva had saved many lives—including her Grandmother's—with her innovative design!

The rabbits returned to tend to their families, the injured, and the lost. While the decoy warren was mostly destroyed, the real Warren sustained limited damage to the main entrance. The decoy had served its purpose, making it difficult for the predators to locate the main entrance and buying time for most of the rabbits to escape. Most of the losses had come from rabbits trapped in tunnels or those slow to emerge from the main exit; the escape tunnels had saved hundreds who otherwise would have been in danger.

The estimated loss was ten percent; this was far fewer than the reported losses from other communities. The somber reality was that the threat was real, and protective actions were valuable in preventing massive destruction. It was a sad day, but a day of gratitude as well for Eva and her team. The Warren had survived!

Decoding the Parable

Let's explore the parable with the CLEAR Change Method. The Warren realized the strategic goal to protect their home, with relatively fewer losses as compared to other warrens under attack. They learned how to create a protective barrier—a new concept to the community—from the Beaver. The bold idea of interconnected burrows for flexible escape routes presented a potential privacy issue, resolved to an acceptable level through innovative thinking and demonstration. The conflict, however, was inconsistent Leadership; some Council leaders were supportive, others wanted to reallocate critical resources to other projects, while Randall (the head bunny) was buying time to find another solution. Our project leader, Eva, had to observe, interpret, and address the inconsistent messages and actions of the Leadership. Only then could she influence, with clear Contrast and Experiences, to *make it easy* for Randall to commit, hold himself and other leaders accountable, and model the needed change behaviors.

Contrast—define the change to be realized, show the value of the change (From This, To That, and Why)

- New predators had emerged and reportedly attacked (and even eliminated) other Warrens in the area. The Warren had to establish proactive measures to save the community from a similar fate. The Warren moved from a position of being a certain victim to being protected.

Leadership—engage formal and informal leaders, understanding interest, influence, and impact

- Randall was the formal leader, with high levels of influence and impact, but was hindered by his need to be the expert in order to be interested or invested.
- The Council had several players, each with differing levels of interest, influence, and impact. This is common in change initiatives! Understanding and managing each leader is a key skill for change leadership. Action steps include providing experiences to engage those who are uncertain and mitigating the impact of those who are resistant.
- Because Randall was uncomfortable with conflict, he did not help manage the actions of the other Council members, especially those actions that distracted from

the life-saving protection project. Recall the Council member who continued to bring up overcrowding, the same Council member who reallocated the experienced builders to the Warren expansion project! This action jeopardized the main project's schedule and safety; to our knowledge, Randall did not address this distraction and poor leadership behavior.

- Leadership modeling new behaviors is key to adoption by the community. Grandmother was an informal influencer with the Elders, as well as a mentor for Eva. Early in the project, Randall's behaviors were superficial. Once the threat was validated by the refugees and the escape routes were demonstrated, Randall gained the confidence to model his support actively and authentically. He modeled his support (and new behaviors) by sponsoring the practice drill, reinforcing the need for preparation to survive.

Experiences – architect experiences to make it easy to do the new thing the right way

- The key experience is the demonstration of the escape tunnels, creating understanding and adoption. This experience validated the escape tunnels in real time and, perhaps more importantly, mitigated the privacy concerns for the Elders and the Council.

- Project prioritization is experiential—the most important projects are resourced and discussed. Although Eva's project was "top priority," resources were diverted to Randall's pet project. The true priority only shifted to Eva's project when Randall placed the focus on issue resolution, progress discussions, and demonstrations of the new tunnel structure across the community.
- Establishing a practice drill for the Warren enabled each rabbit to practice the new escape process under simulated conditions. The opportunities to practice in a safe environment, to test the new process, and to learn new skills are key experiences for engagement and successful implementation. Enabling people to learn how to do the new thing the right way shows investment in their success, improving the probability of the organization's success.
- Creating specific experiences for resistant leaders demonstrates the commitment to alignment; combining the experience with responsibility makes the change more difficult to ignore or refute. Within the parable, the assignment of the resistant Council members to measure the exit rate during the practice drill called on these leaders to acknowledge the speed achieved with the new structure as well as a front-row

seat to the explosion of rabbits exiting from the new tunnels. What a sight!

Accountability—establish clear roles and ownership for the planned elements and outcomes

- The big challenge for Eva was the passive accountability (or lack of accountability) from Randall. She had to address his behavior, and did so in a private conversation that established trust and allowed Randall to reset his position without public embarrassment. Influencing individuals in leadership positions effectively can be uncomfortable. We often assume our leaders are fully informed and accountable, which may not be the case; communicating specific expectations to those in positions of authority is critical. Just think about the fable of the Emperor's New Clothes: imagine a respected leader (the Emperor) who thought he was wearing the latest in high fashion but was completely naked. As the story goes, everyone thought he knew what he was doing and didn't dare question his choice, when in fact he had been misled and misinformed, resulting in great embarrassment. Why didn't anyone tell the Emperor he wasn't wearing any clothes? Similarly, why don't we tell our leaders what we need them to do and when, re-engaging them in the change initiative? Even with Accountability, we need to make it easy for our leaders to do the right thing.

Reinforcement—reinforce the desired outcomes and celebrate interim successes, drive to the finish line

- Eva's phased approach enables focus and celebration of early wins throughout the project. For example, Phase One allowed acknowledgement of the decoy warren completion, with the demonstration / pilot of the escape tunnels celebrated as a unique milestone. Progress updates reinforce the project progression and create the opportunity to discuss barriers, distractions, and accountability concerns.
- The daily Warren meetings were a means of reinforcement, most effective once the commitment to the project had been established.
- Learning from the experiences of the refugees confirmed and named the predators, reinforcing the reality of the threat. The experience of the practice drill helped reinforce the need to respond with urgency.

Discussion Questions

- Why was Eva's relationship with the Beaver important to the project?
- What actions indicated the leadership support was in question? How did Eva learn about the inconsistencies?
- How did Randall try to appear supportive when he was actually doubting?
- What lesson did Grandmother teach Eva about leadership styles?
- What value was informal leadership vs formal leadership throughout the project?
- Was the outcome a success or a failure?

Discussion Questions (with Answers)

- Why was Eva's relationship with the Beaver important to the project?

The Beaver provided expertise on predator abatement. Eva applied this key learning in designing protection from a new type of predator.

- What actions indicated the leadership support was in question? How did Eva learn about the inconsistencies?

Reassignment of the expert builders to another project signaled a competing priority and resistance to the plan Eva had put forward. Eva learned about the reassignment indirectly, after the fact—further signaling resistance and dismissal of Eva's leadership role.

- How did Randall try to appear supportive when he was actually doubting?

Randall communicated support in public, with forced rhetoric as recognition. He placed his actions (or lack of corrective actions) as priorities, and Eva's plans were ignored, sending confusing signals to the Leadership team and encouraging them to continue with non-supportive behaviors.

- What lesson did Grandmother teach Eva about leadership styles?

Grandmother helped Eva understand Randall's experiences and expertise as his motivation for action, as well as how to create new experiences to help move Randall along his own change journey for the good of the Warren.

- What value was informal leadership vs formal leadership throughout the project?

The Warren culture emphasized formal leadership, but informal leadership was far more impactful. Grandmother is an informal leader, both as Eva's mentor and as the influencer with the Elders. Eva did not hold a formal leadership position on the Council, yet her influence over Randall and over the Warren was significant.

- Was the outcome a success or a failure?

As we contemplate the overall survival of the Warren as a success, a 10 percent loss of life to a predator could be considered a failure. However, it was a higher survival rate than it would have been had Eva's plan not been put into place.

Application Questions

- How might you explore innovative ideas from other businesses / organizations, like Eva did with the Beaver?
- Who are the quietly resistant leaders in your organization? How do they distract from the articulated priorities to serve their own priorities?
- What are the proactive protective actions you are implementing?
- What cultural norms are unspoken (or overt) barriers to implementing innovative change?

- How are you supporting the leaders engaged in program implementation? How are you celebrating early wins along with an urgent implementation?
- As a leader, how are you facilitating or driving deliberate dialogue to resolve differing priorities and ensuring alignment toward the strategic vision?
- Randall held a bias for his own expertise. What biases exist in your organization that cause you to ignore or dismiss a new threat? A new disruptive opportunity?

I hope you have enjoyed these three parables and the lessons shared by wise leaders in the animal kingdom. Stories in hand, let's dig into the details of the CLEAR Change method.

Please swim, buzz, or hop across the Clover Meadow to Section 2, the technical stuff.

SECTION 2:

CLEAR Change
The Technical Stuff

"There is nothing so stable as change."

—Bob Dylan, songwriter

Change is inevitable. Markets evolve and shift. Customers respond to novel products, demanding constant innovation. Employees demand more from employers, with the power to choose as the workforce shifts in age, flexibility, and skillsets. Driving change through your organization is essential for survival and success, yet it can be overwhelming. In addition, studies show 70 percent of business-based change initiatives fail (Kotter 2012). Change is necessary, but intimidating, as it presents a high degree of difficulty and low probability of success. The most responsive will survive—but how?

Welcome to the CLEAR Change Method.

The CLEAR Change Method is a simple and straightforward framework that is easy to maneuver and scalable for the size of any change initiative. This necessary architecture is proven to increase your probability of success.

After 30+ years in the corporate industry driving start-ups, process improvement, and large-scale change, I have leveraged my experiences and observations to develop this framework for driving successful change. Where 70 percent of change initiatives fail, I have cataloged an 82 percent *SUCCESS* rate over more than 25 engagements in the past seven years.

I've met with leaders across manufacturing, financial services, and tech start-ups. I've interviewed change leaders in not-for-profits, churches, school systems, health care service providers, and universities. As we shared the stories of successful change initiatives, the CLEAR Change Method applied time and time again. And as we discussed those initiatives that failed, patterns emerged with consistent points of failure that the CLEAR Change Method would have addressed. I've incorporated several case studies in each chapter of this section, providing real-world evidence of the method. For each chapter, I've presented a successful application and a not-so-successful example—and all names have been changed, of course!

Consider your own change journey as you read, mapping your journey with the CLEAR Change Method in each chapter. The tools and templates presented in the book are easy to replicate and use. The CLEAR Change Guidebook and the tools and templates are also available for download at www.clearchangebook.com.

THE CLEAR CHANGE MODEL

"If you don't like something, change it. If you can't change it, change your attitude."

—Maya Angelou, poet

Change is part of business. Strategic change can drive great value if implemented well—it can create new tools, capabilities, services, or products, which become an essential part of our everyday life. Leaders do not create change efforts for the sake of change, just to see what might happen. Change initiatives are developed by experienced, capable leaders to realize strategic outcomes and top-level performance.

While we seem to recognize the importance of change, only 28 percent of all change initiatives deliver the necessary change (Jacquemont, Maor and Reich 2019). With all this value and capability, how is it possible so many change initiatives fail?

We can categorize change failure into three practical failure modes:

- Failure to See: the desired change is not understood or valued by those involved
- Failure to Move: the change is understood and valued, but individuals have difficulty moving to the new process, perspective, or place; they don't know how to act differently or can't break free of the current state
- Failure to Adopt: individuals are able to move to the new state, but they lose traction or interest and default back to the comfort and ease of the former state; change is abandoned for loss of interest or perceived value

In understanding how systems fail, we can address the inherent failure modes proactively and increase our probability of success. Across my years of application experience on start-up projects, process-improvement programs, and strategic-change initiatives, a consistent pattern of successful elements emerged that combatted all three failure modes and drove change initiatives to success with a high rate of achievement. The architecture I derived is the CLEAR Change Method.

The CLEAR Change Method is comprised of five key elements:

C = Contrast	**Define the change to be realized,** compare your current state to the desired future state, and articulate the value of the change (From This, To That, and Why) This is the core of the change initiative, influencing every other element and phase of the journey
L = Leadership	**Engage leaders**—both formal and informal—into the need to change and the value to be realized
E = Experiences	**Architect experiences for all** leaders, doers, and users that introduce the change and define how we might make it easy to do the new thing the right way. This is the biggest factor in the change journey!
A = Accountability	**Establish clear roles and ownership** for the planned actions and outcomes. This element ensures execution of Experiences and progress along the journey.
R = Reinforcement	**Reinforce the desired outcomes** and celebrate interim successes and progress toward the finish line. Remembering and recognizing the milestones along the journey of change helps individuals accept and adopt the new normal, sustaining the desired change.

The CLEAR elements are tightly related, addressing failure modes of change with both individual and collective focus.

As described in the definitions above, Contrast is the core of the change initiative. Contrast is the target, addressing the Failure to See, and is leveraged in every other element. To address the Failure to Move, we engage Leadership as a group and create lasting Experiences for individuals. To address Failure to Adopt, we use ownership and commitment for individual Accountability and Reinforcement for regular recognition of overall progress.

In this section of the book, we will explore each of the CLEAR Change Method elements with the following structure:

- Definition of the CLEAR Change element
- Details, including tools and templates to explore each element for application to any change initiative

- Keys for Success, highlighting 2–3 essential actions
- Pitfalls, including potential issues to anticipate and mitigate
- Case Studies of successful and not-so-successful change initiatives with specific details outlined in the element's context

Now that you have a high-level view, let's begin your journey. What change are you trying to achieve?

C IS FOR CONTRAST

"People are very open-minded about new things—as long as they're exactly like the old ones."

—Charles Kettering, inventor

The heart of any change initiative is the change itself.

As you establish the case for change, communicating Contrast helps create visibility and understanding among all involved. Contrast is the difference between the current state we're in and the future state we want to move to, as well as the explanation as to why we want to get there.

By using Contrast, we can determine what needs to change to achieve success in the future state. We can also build the case for change—the reason why we want to change—with shared understanding, alignment, and readiness to move forward across the organization.

Details: Contrast

We all experience many deliberate changes in life, such as a move, as well as changes that are not within our control, such as the weather. As we consider leading a change for improvement in a business strategy, there are three key components that help us describe and define the change, using Contrast:

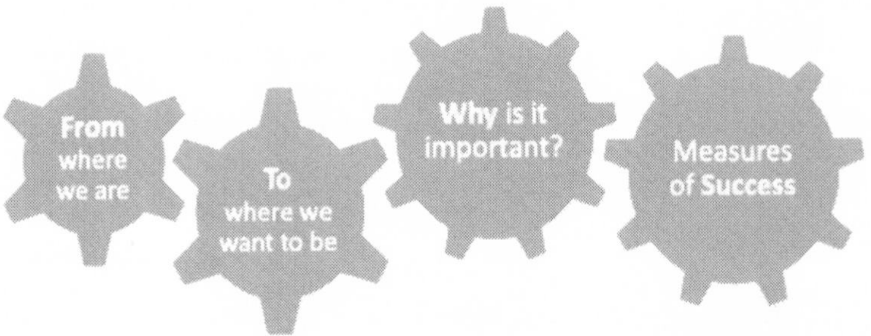

Depicted as gears, the elements of Contrast are interconnected, aligned, and must all be in place for movement forward.

- From-To: For any change, there is a starting point and an endpoint. These states of being must be different, and that difference must be obvious.
- Why: For any change, you must have a compelling rationale, a statement that explains why the change is worth it.
- Measures of Success: For any change, we must articu-

late the expected benefits of the change in measurable terms. Success measures can be about the outcome, but also ought to establish attributes of the end state.

This seems straightforward and easy to execute—and it can be. You may already know your Why, defined by the organizational mission or vision, but you don't have the From-To. You may have the From-To, resulting from customer feedback or regulatory audit, but you don't have clear Measures of Success. The point is, you need all three elements of Contrast to successfully engage and motivate the organization. Change is not a mystery, but it is a process that is often shortchanged. Moving strategically requires research and time to reflect. In other words, change requires vision.

From-To

Communicating the value of change requires a description of the journey, starting with where you are today (From) and where you want to go (To). Let's consider the From—To for each of the parables:

- Parable 1: The Knight must cross from one side of the raging river to the other side as quickly as possible; the Knight must learn to swim.
- Parable 2: The EllerBee hive must find a path from low productivity due to limited resources to higher productivity.

- Parable 3: The Warren must shift from unprotected to protected in the face of a new predator.

When defining the From-To statements with clients, we start with a standard suite of questions:

- What do our customers value today? What would delight our customers beyond imagination?
- What pains do our customers experience? What pains do they accept as unchangeable?
- What advantages or gains could we provide our customers that they could not achieve with our competitors?
- What advantages or gains do our competitors provide better than we do?
- How will the changing business environment impact our business?
- In each case, why do we want to change?
- In each case, what does success look like? How do we measure success?

These are not easy questions to address. The discussion can be organized within the Contrast Development template, with an example extracted from the NewBees parable:

Contrast Development	From: where we are today?	To: where we want to go?	Why do we want to change?	How do we measure success?
What do our customers value? What value is beyond imagination?	our hive needs more food with our flight radius	bountiful food supply and space for all – 2 hives are better than 1!	with overcrowding and limited food, we will not all survive	- ample food supply within flight - room for everybee in a hive - high production rates in each hives
What pains do our customers experience? Accept as unchangeable?				
What advantage or gains could we provide better than our competition?				
What advantage or gains does our competition provide better than we do?				
How will the changing business environment impact our business?				

Once you have brainstormed the From-To responses specific to your customers and business environment, consider the Why. Is there a compelling Why that addresses many of the From-To statements? Is there a strategic goal to achieve, a specific purpose aligned to your change initiative? For instance, are your customer reviews indicating a lack of customer service? If so, what are the consequences of not understanding and addressing the issues? If you were to improve the customer experience, would you see an increase in repeat business? Would it differentiate you from your competitors? The From-To discussion helps you define a compelling Why.

The Why

The motivational element of the Contrast statement is the Why. With a compelling Why, the reason for change can be seen and understood, mitigating the Failure to See.

The Why can be a giant leap or a small step forward. In business, small change is quite valuable in process improvement or regulated industries. For a professional athlete, performance improves with a small change in stance, angle, or hand position; small changes yield big results. You may have many Whys for your change initiative; a change to focus on social responsibility, for example, could result in expanded business *and* a sense of purpose for your employees. With complimentary Why statements, be honest with their relative importance—you may need to make tradeoffs as the plan develops.

We often think of the reason for change on a grand scale. In the parables, change was essential to the survival of a community—they each had a critical purpose: the Knight's Why was to save the Castle, Eva's Why was to save the Warren from destruction. Here are a few more examples of highly valued and unquestionable Why statements you may find are motivating your potential change:

- To Save Ourselves—from death, from closure, from takeover
- For Child Welfare—to create a better life, rescue from poverty, hunger, abuse
- To Save the Planet—climate change, pollution, loss of natural resources, alien invasion
- For World Peace—for activists, political leaders, and beauty pageant winners
- To Make Boatloads of Money

While the last one doesn't fit with the humanit of the others, it is the most recognized. It may sour but product disruptors, service providers, restaurants, games, and conveniences are all products designed by the founders/ owners to make money as their primary Why.

Measures of Success

Success must be defined in terms you can measure. It is the expected benefit, differential performance indicator, or revenue needed for solvency. Ask your team: *What does Success look like?*

Making money is the most measurable way to determine success on the list. Certainly, we'd like to improve the health and wellbeing of children, but how do we measure our success on that front? The timeline to affect change on a global level is long and arduous; moving the needle on any one indicator is complex and confounded by many factors. Noting that you have achieved the goal of raising $1,000 for a charity that helps children is more measurable than trying to weigh global childhood health, and can help motivate and encourage your team to actually work toward that goal.

Your Why is essential to motivate, but so are your measures by which victory—or at least success—will be declared.

Adding it Up

At this point, you may be overwhelmed. Defining (and surviving) change is hard! You're right, it's a lot to process.

Some of you are starting with a blank page. Many of you have been handed a change initiative out of the blue, resulting from competitor challenges, market dynamics, or your vice president who just read a business book and has a great idea. In any of these scenarios, asking questions about where you are today, where you want to go, why you or your customer care, and how to measure success, is *the* place to start!

Create your own grid, have a brainstorming session, ask people on the street. Distill what you have learned, felt, and debated into the Contrast statement that best represents your change initiative:

> *We are moving* ***from*** *[our current state]* **to** *[our future state] because it is important to [****Why****], and we will know we have succeeded when we [****measure of success****].*

Here is the completed Contrast statement for each of the parables presented in Section 1.

- The Knight must learn to swim to cross from one side of the raging river to the other side as quickly as possible to save the Castle and the villagers from the Wolves. The Knight will succeed if the Knight reaches the Village before the Wolves with enough time to prepare and ultimately defeat the Wolves.
- The EllerBee hive must find a path from low productivi-

ty due to limited resources to higher productivity to ensure the colony's survival. The Squadron will succeed if they locate a new food source within reach of the current hive. Because this was not achievable, the Squadron redefined success: the NewBees will succeed if they establish a new highly productive hive with ample resources as well as reduce the burden on resources in the EllerBee hive, promoting a return to higher productivity.

- The Warren must shift from unprotected to protected in the face of a new predator to survive. The Warren will succeed if the predators are prevented from attacking or, if they do attack, the community survival rate is greater than 80 percent (knowing other Warrens lost more than 80 percent of their population).

Your Contrast statement communicates the value of the change, the difficulty of the change, and sets the journey in motion.

Keys for Success: Contrast

- Be authentic, be logical, and be realistic every step of the way: From here To there, Why we are doing it, and how we Measure Success.
- Establish Measures of Success that reflect the destination (To this) of the Contrast statement and the realities of your business.

Pitfalls in Contrast

If you can't communicate Contrast clearly, the change won't happen. It's as simple as that.

Without a simple, intentional, relatable Contrast statement of From-To, Why, and Measures of Success, the change stalls with a Failure to See. In this failure mode, the individuals asked to do something different (to change) don't see the value in deviating from what they know to do. They may not understand or accept that doing something differently will actually drive them toward success.

We can state Failure to See in several ways:

- The change is too complicated, too difficult, too aggressive
- I'm not affected, so I don't need to understand it
- I don't see how this change gets us to our end goal—it's not logical
- I don't understand what you're trying to accomplish
- What's in it for me?
- I'm missing it—why are we doing this?

Have you ever been involved in a meeting about strategic or organizational change and had the question "what's the point?" sneak into your brain? Perhaps you theoretically understood the rationale for a change initiative, but you were not sure of the desired outcome or definition of success. Or, worse yet, maybe after a change was made, the end result did not measure up to the intended improvement.

If this sounds familiar, you have Failed to See. This wasn't necessarily your fault. Odds are, the leader communicating the desired change to you has not followed the process of the change well enough, or simply has not explained the Contrast effectively.

Each component of Contrast is required to move forward. Because change involves emotions, it must have a motivational force. If the aim is to save the planet, for example, the Contrast statement must be actionable, must have a logical outcome, and must measure success tied to saving the planet; if the logic isn't obvious, the change initiative will not make sense, and the organization will not have the motivation to move forward.

Similarly, if Leadership uses the same vague Why statement, time and time again, the logic may hold water, but the credibility and motivation is lost over time. In the NewBees parable, if the Why was stated as "to be more efficient" or "to be more comfortable," the Squadron might not have pushed beyond the flight boundary and never have discovered the Clover Meadow.

Similarly, influencers may deploy the stalling tactic "We've tried this before" or "It can't be that bad; let's wait to see what really happens," regardless of the Contrast statement's motivation. We heard this from Randall and other Council members in the parable of the Warren; it wasn't until refugees from another community described the predator's attack that Randall could see the real threat. We'll discuss this issue more in the next sections on Leadership and Experiences. First, let's look at a case study demonstrating an effective Contrast statement and successful change initiative.

Case Study 1: Grades vs Learning

Many mid-sized communities are investing in holistic wellness programming to improve health factors for the current residents, as well as to attract growing numbers of new residents. Schools play a critical role in the wellbeing of students, teachers, and the community.

As the principal of a nationally ranked high school, Ethan questioned whether grades were reflective of the wellbeing of the student, specifically the learning or mastery of the topic. The answer was, as suspected, *not entirely*.

With the help of a focused team, Ethan's team defined Contrast for their new state as follows:

- From-To: move From a culture of Grades To a culture of Learning
- Why: Students who graduate from our school system must be educated and prepared for the next phase of life. Focus on learning and performance within a subject is far more impactful and durable than grades.
- Measures of Success:

    - Assessment tools are used as a means of learning and for demonstrating learning/mastery; the result is knowledge, not a grade.
    - A defined retake/retest process to provide oppor-

tunities to learn and demonstrate learning. The grade can be updated as learning and mastery is achieved.

- Eliminate grades for non-essential work—for example, extra credit points for bringing in shared supplies (like Kleenex or glue sticks) were no longer acceptable

By redefining the assessment principles and clarifying expectations, the teachers could understand and implement the needed changes. The strategic statement of Contrast—the From-To, Why, and Measures of Success—was challenging, as it represented a deep cultural shift for teachers, students, and parents. Because the old grading norms had been present in everyday activities, the change was hard to execute consistently. Buy-in was most difficult on the small things—no extra credit for bringing in supplies was a challenge!

Ethan invested in each teacher's journey with consistent coaching and discussion, and has been pleased with the progress toward successful adoption. Ethan regularly reinforced the measures of success and rationale, as they resonated with teachers, ensuring the school was preparing their students to succeed in the next phase of life, be it college, military, or employment.

The journey to a culture of learning is not yet complete. Progress has been consistent and successful, and students are better prepared for post-high-school success, as reported by recent graduates.

****

In the next case study, the Contrast statement doesn't quite measure up. What changes would you recommend to improve the Contrast statement?

Case Study 2: Let's All Work Together

Howard was an accomplished scientist and respected leader in his industry. His quick wit, technically challenging questions, and brilliant insights differentiated him in the world of software development in healthcare. Each leader on his team was equally accomplished and showed strong commitment to the technical focus of their area, while enjoying a bit of good-natured competition among each other.

Over time, that good-natured competition became less and less "good-natured." Each leader grew to believe their area was most impactful to the overall business. Howard recognized this competition was becoming an issue, as the battle for new products across the industry would require cross-technical development and disruptive designs. His team needed to be working together and building one another up, not tearing each other down so their own work looked better in comparison.

Howard's team needed to learn to work together. This was Howard's first attempt at filling out the contrast statement:

- From-To: Move From functional products To integrated multi-functional products.
- Why: Industry trends and customer needs suggested more comprehensive solutions with reduced resources on a rapid timeline. (Not very compelling, especial-

ly with current successes in functionally developed products.)

- Measures of Success: "working together." (Far too vague. This is where it really falls apart for Howard.)

Howard empowered his three top leaders to figure out how best to work together, which projects would advance this new way of working, and the impact on resources and timeline.

Because the organization measured each individual annually on the success of the projects already in progress and tied business planning resources to the near-term needs of these projects, the opportunity to develop multi-functional products was routinely put off to the next round of product decisions, even with the new goal in place. As sales went down and resources became more limited, the level of need (and noise) from each individual leader to develop functional products became more pronounced and no multi-functional products were developed.

A more compelling Contrast statement could be:

We are moving from functional products to integrated multi-functional products to provide life-changing solutions to our customers. We will know we have succeeded when we initiate three multi-functional designs in the next quarter, with launch and target sales growth of 25 percent next year to replace declining sales across our functional product portfolio.

With this Contrast statement, "Let's All Work Together" might have become a reinforcing mantra representing the inherent success of collaborating to deliver life-changing products to customers. Without a compelling Contrast statement and leadership buy-in, it instead became a cynical catchphrase, and the teams drifted even further apart, entrenched in their siloed mindset.

****

Contrast facilitates communication, building understanding, and increased engagement in the case for change. Contrast makes the change visible. An effective Contrast statement includes From-To, a compelling Why, and Measures of Success.

Once we have established Contrast, it is important to engage others on the journey. Let's start with engaging the Leadership of the organization.

L IS FOR LEADERSHIP

"If you're going to change things, you have to be with the people who hold the levers."

—Ruth Bader Ginsburg, Supreme Court Justice

In the Leadership element of our CLEAR Change Method, we will deliberately engage leaders—both formal and informal—with the need for change, learn how to model change for others, and understand how to realize the value of the change at hand.

Details: Leadership

Each organization is built on hierarchy, spoken or unspoken, with decisions made at the appropriate level in the structure. Formal leadership—the Boss, if you will—has the responsibility to manage resources, assign work, measure performance, and establish and disband teams, projects, and strategies. Any successful change initiative must have support (or tolerance) from the leadership of the impacted organization.

But selling the Boss on the next brilliant strategy isn't enough. We need much more than the top of the org chart to play this game!

Leadership is more than the act of supervising others or managing an organization. Leadership, at its core, is the ability to influence outcomes through people and their actions. Leadership is a skillset, a series of actions, a covert process that harnesses the current of change.

How lovely. If only it always worked that way!

As you probably know, in many cases, Leadership modifies or blocks the flow of change with swift, silent, unquestionable diversions. A predominant failure point for change is the lack of key Leadership support, manifesting as a Failure to Move (the change is understood and valued, but individuals have difficulty moving to the future state) across the organization. If the right leaders aren't on board, the change initiative will not be valued, will not move forward and will not succeed.

If Contrast is the map for a change initiative, Leaders are the navigators. When the Leadership team is on course to realize the desired change, the organization moves forward. If the Leadership team is not aligned with the change or with each other, the organization may stop to ask for directions or consider detours. The organization fails to move.

How do we engage leaders—the *right* leaders? It starts with knowing who the key leaders are, both formal and informal. Ask yourself the following questions:

- Who owns the process, technology, system, or product that is proposed to change? Consider organizational leaders and functional or technical leaders.
- Who are the experts in developing or executing the process, technology, system, or product to be changed?
- Who are the formal leaders of the organization impacted by the change? Consider 2–3 levels, including the leader who manages those directly affected.
- Who are the downstream recipients of the process, technology, system, or product proposed to change? Consider both formal organizational leaders and experts/owners.
- Are there implications or needs for change with upstream suppliers or processes? Consider these leaders, experts, and owners.
- Finally, who are the experts or informal leaders directly impacted by the change? Who are the hidden influencers (at any level) who have history and knowledge?

Now that you have a list of potential Leaders to consider, you can assess how each individual might support or detract from the change initiative. To make this assessment, we have created the Leadership Assessment Tool below.

Specifically, we assess the 3 I's:

- Interest—Is the individual interested in the change initiative? Does he/she care? Does he/she have an interest in successful implementation?
- Influence—Does the individual have influence over the resources necessary to carry out the change journey? These resources may be people, technology, equipment, governance processes, funding, performance measures, etc.
- Impact—Does the change impact the individual's work performance or organization? Does the change impact the individual's status or expertise?

We can simply evaluate each characteristic as favorable (aligned with the change program), not favorable (resistant or against the change program), or neutral with points assigned accordingly. Here is an example one of my teams used:

Rating	Points
Awesome	2
Supportive	1
Non-Committal	0
Contrary	-1
Destructive	-2

These are descriptive terms on a linear scale; higher positive scores show alignment and support for the change, negative scores indicate resistance or opposition. You can use whatever terms work for you—the Awesome to Destructive scale fit the cultural swings we were feeling at the time. Some groups are satisfied with Very Positive/Positive/Neutral/Negative/Very Negative; use what works for you and your team.

A completed Leadership Assessment Grid might look like this:

	Interest	Influence	Impact	Total	Notes
Randall	-1	1	2	3	reluctant!
Eva	2	0	2	4	
Grandmother	1	2	2	5	secret weapon
Council Member focused on overcrowding	-2	-1	-2	-5	destructive

During the assessment discussion, make notes on the grid (as in the example above) to add context to the score; in the example, we see Randall has a somewhat positive score, but we know he is reluctantly using his influence to move forward to buy time for a better solution.

Once the assessment is complete, you have broader insight into who might be supportive, who has concerns, and who may not know enough. You will then have a clearer picture on who needs to be leveraged, who needs to be heard, and who needs more convincing.

Follow up with leaders who were neutral (category score of 0) on the assessment grid with discussions to engage them with the case for change. Schedule specific discussions with leaders who scored low on the assessment grid (negative on any category score or total <3). These discussions will likely surface important perspectives and concerns to address, mitigate, or accept. These targeted discussions may help you raise their assessment numbers—and, therefore, support levels.

Discussions also help you identify leaders or experts you may not have considered—these could be underground influencers who surface as the program progresses; for example, the Farmer in Parable 2 is an unknown influencer for the NewBee colony. It's better to engage these players early, listen to them, and understand how they align.

The assessment tool provides a means to prioritize conversations and engagement with the leaders identified. The knowledge gained in Leadership discussions will inform the Experiences you construct and concerns or barriers to address. Invest time early in the process to understand the Leadership and their positions.

Keys for Success: Leadership

- Take the time to be comprehensive in your Leadership list

- Engage Leaders in ongoing discussions to build support and consider concerns

Pitfalls in Leadership

In my leadership interviews exploring change initiatives across industries, Leadership engagement was the most-cited reason for failure. Here are a few pitfalls to consider:

- Building Leadership Engagement Takes Time

Even once you have a good list of Leaders, know that you're far from done. It takes time to connect with each of the Leaders identified. Craft discussions to better understand each Leader's perspective, impact on their organization, and support for the desired change.

It's easy to fill out the Leadership Assessment grid based on past experiences or reputation, but this is a risky game! The context behind the ratings is most helpful when it is specific to the current environment and proposed change initiative. A Leader who was helpful and invested in a previous initiative might resist this one, and vice versa. Take the time to understand and assess the Leadership to ensure alignment, address concerns, define value, and create consistent messages for shared use.

- Leaders Don't Know How

Leaders may be reluctant or resistant to move forward with the change initiative due to a lack of knowledge, skills, or time to learn. The pressures to deliver on schedule with limited resources are ever-present; the proposed change initiative presents unacceptable interruptions or uncertainty in a world that demands accountability. Admitting a gap in skills or knowledge is difficult. Engage each leader to better understand the proposed change's specific impact on their organization, and design a way to help bridge the gap in skills or knowledge across all involved.

- Leaders Don't Feel Valued

As often seen in TV dramas, a disgruntled or overlooked leader may sabotage the effort. This is an extreme position, but it can happen when stakes are high. I've worked with technical experts who would allow (or even help) a project fail so they could swoop in as the hero to save the day. Identifying the hidden influencers is the first step; engaging them as valued contributors to the project results is critical for the organization to move forward.

- Leaders Don't "Walk the Walk"

Change can present political and organizational changes, some of which may not be well understood or anticipated at the onset. Leaders who feel negatively affected by the change may present challenges at key milestones, exposing additional concerns or unexpected barriers. These Leaders also communicate mixed messages, supporting the project publicly but resisting or denouncing the project in side conversations. In the Warren parable, Randall voiced support for the proposed plans and the implementation leader, Eva; however, he was not authentic in his support, allowing other leaders to reassign key resources while he pursued alternative solutions to the issue. Randall's inconsistent actions and messages cast doubt on the project, undermining the priority and impact of the initiative. The mixed-message Leader enables doubt, resulting in an organizational Failure to Move.

It's not practical to expect an entire leadership team to be on board with a proposed change initiative, especially not at the outset. Understanding Leadership positions and concerns in context of the change allows for proactive planning and Experiences to mitigate the Failure to Move at both the Leadership and organizational levels. Let's explore two more case studies to better understand the impact of Leadership.

Case Study 3: Priestly Practice

In Spring of 2018, I had the honor of interviewing Father Brian, a leader for liturgy and worship in Iowa, about a very impactful and wide-sweeping change. After several years of study and work, the Catholic Church had finalized the third edition of the Roman Missal, the text supporting the Catholic mass. This edition employed a different translation method, presenting a more formal equivalence to ancient text as translated into English.

The revised version of the missal affected several familiar and frequently spoken prayers and responses. For example, the priest offers *Peace be with you,* and the response changed from a conversational response, *and also with you,* to the revised response, *and with your spirit.* The shift is important, and as Father Brian explained to me: the revised response acknowledges the presence of the Holy Spirit, a key element of the Trinity in Christian beliefs. Upon reflection, the more familiar response is exactly that—too familiar, missing the original intention of the exchange.

These prayers and responses had been in place for more than 40 years—ingrained into the memory of parishioners for as long as the mass had celebrated in English. In addition to presenting some ambitious language (*born of the Fathe*r became *consubstantial with the Father,* for example), it was a translation that differed from the version preferred by many in the US leadership of the Church. In some cases, the local and regional leadership felt powerless; once the decision on the translation had been made, the debate was over.

As the leader for liturgy and worship across the Archdiocese (a large region led by a bishop, spanning a major metropolitan area or state), the responsibility for a sound and effective implementation plan for the community fell to Father Brian. Ever the optimist, Father Brian described the assignment as "choosing the best of the imperfect and running with it." Local oversight for implementation of the new version presented an opportunity to take a pragmatic approach to when and how, leveraging the implementation to enrich celebration of the faith. Father Brian focused his efforts on the most important stakeholders—the parish priests, the leaders of the church communities they serve.

A parish priest is the formal leader of a church community, celebrating mass and leading operations with both religious and lay staff at one to three churches in a specific location, defined as a parish. These priests needed to prepare and commit to implementing the revised missal within the prescribed overall timeline, with the specific timeline for each parish to be determined based on the needs and readiness of the parish.

Father Brian could have taken the easy road, handing the task over to each parish priest, perhaps sharing resources as requested. Instead, Father Brian took the opportunity for engagement across this essential yet often independent leadership team.

Father Brian gathered the priests from across the Archdiocese into small groups, asking them to spend a full eight-hour day together to discuss the changes and implementation. This was a novel experience for many of the participants! Although they serve parishes in close proximity, there are few opportunities to meet together for collegial or liturgical discussion.

The sessions were powerful, as each priest was asked to share how they each learned how to say the mass. Each had different experiences, some learning at an early age as an altar server, some learning later in the seminary. With the common construction and centralized management of how the mass is celebrated, the range of experiences was an interesting surprise. The priests also shared their core beliefs and feelings about the mass, including what was essential to retain, and what they feared might be lost in the changes. All recognized and discussed how celebrating mass is the central experience of their faith.

In sharing what they believed and valued most about the mass, the priests moved from reluctance to shared and collaborative posture. Each priest held ownership for the timeframe and necessary resources for implementation in their own parish, providing the flexibility to implement as appropriate. With attention to leadership discussion and experiential learning, the parish priests now shared a common understanding and deeper community connection.

****

The next case study explores what can happen when you don't have a full understanding of influential leaders.

Case Study 4: New Math

Charlotte is an experienced and well-respected middle school principal in a highly rated public school system. She is a successful innovator, recognized for championing a series of successful programs benefiting both students and teachers.

Charlotte actively engages her teachers, often coordinating small teams to understand and assess recent trends in education. In this spirit, a team of math teachers formed to explore potential curriculum changes for improved outcomes across the system's twin middle schools. The team identified a digital learning platform that aligned with the curriculum requirements and state standards.

Applying a digital platform within the classroom would allow the students to progress at an individual pace, reflective of their skills and demonstrated learning. Teachers would manage the classroom differently, providing much more personalized help to students. This would allow for additional help for some students and opportunity for higher-level challenges for advanced students. The data presented by the platform would allow teachers to focus lectures on individuals, small groups, or on the entire class. For those students who have a high aptitude for math, the platform would allow them to progress at a more rapid pace, challenging them with the next subject as fast as mastery was demonstrated.

The math platform leveraged the full capability of the school's recently implemented 1:1 laptop program, while engaging students with a tailored-learning solution. Charlotte supported the grassroots initiative with the Administration and provided needed resources and communication channels for a successful implementation.

Based on the case study to date, here is the Leadership Assessment grid:

	Interest	**Influence**	**Impact**	**Total**	**Notes**
Principal	2	0	1	3	supportive, teachers take the lead
Middle School Math Teachers	1	2	2	5	empowered!
Parents	1	0	-1	0	don't know how this will work

A few comments on the scores:

- You might think the principal has a great deal of influence on curriculum decisions. In this school system (perhaps many school systems), the principal is a supporting character, empowering the individual department (math, for this case study) to deliver against the school district's curriculum framework and state requirements. As this grass-roots effort was about how to deliver the content and not the curriculum content itself, the teachers were given a great deal of ownership.

- Parents were not aware of the change initiative as it developed, and had no influence on the curriculum or delivery method. They had recently invested in laptops for each of their middle-school-aged children, so more use in coursework meant better use of the investment. In addition, many parents saw laptop integration into coursework as a mirror to their own work environment, thereby preparing students early for their future work environment.
- For parents, the Impact characteristic reflects the impact of the change on their child. Parents who had children well-suited for math and technology saw the move to more online content as a positive impact; those with students who struggled with either math or technology saw online content as a negative impact on their child. The latter group was a greater population, swinging the overall rating to slightly negative.

Let's continue with the case study.

After having been in the digital math class for two years, the pilot group of students graduated from the middle school to the high school. The middle school was ahead of the curve on the 1:1 laptop program, and the high school was still in transition. With some discomfort, the students had to re-acclimate to the traditional lecture/textbook model for high school.

Thanks to the program, several students had progressed beyond the established model; some had already completed Geometry before entering high school, a class normally reserved for sophomores or accelerated freshmen. These students did not struggle as much with re-adapting to pen and paper, but they were bored in their freshman classes and were no longer challenged in the way they were used to.

On the other end of the spectrum, as you might expect, some students had a lot of difficulty adapting. Some students—those who were not well-suited to learning on the digital platform or, alternatively, benefited greatly from the digital platform's individualized teaching—couldn't demonstrate capabilities expected at the high school level.

Once parents entered conferences with high school math teachers to better understand why their son or daughter was struggling with math, one explanation offered—appropriately—was that their student may not have mastered math in middle school. The student's high school grade reflected the gap. An unexpected low math grade was a topic of great concern; every grade counted toward college admissions and scholarships (parents were passionate and enraged in public meetings—yikes!).

With these concerns expressed by parents and the high school math teachers, the administration commissioned an independent review of the middle school online math program. The study focused on the capabilities of students currently in the program and those who had progressed to high school.

The review was inconclusive—there was no deficiency, but also no advantage to the digital math program on its own, and in the greater scheme of things, it was causing problems for many students later on. After a series of discussions with the administration and the school board, the program was discontinued.

As we review the program retrospectively, a more accurate and complete Leadership Assessment grid would look something like this:

	Interest	Influence	Impact	Total
Principal	2	0	1	3
Middle School Math Teachers	1	2	2	5
Middle School Parents	1	0	-1	0
High School Math Teachers	0	-1	-2	-3
High School Parents	0	-2	-2	-4
School District Administrators	0	0	-1	-1

Upon reflection, Charlotte identified the failure point was quite clear: the team failed to identify the *high school* math teachers and parents as informal leaders that would have interest, influence, and see impact with any change implemented at the middle school level. There was an appreciation across the twin middle schools, consideration for the skill base of teachers, accommodation of learning style for students and needs of the parents—but they limited their view to middle school, not considering the downstream effect of middle school students progressing into high school students. Partnership with high school math teachers and a collaborative review of the program could have addressed concerns related to high school coursework, created a more deliberate transition plan for students, and would have allowed the high school teachers to engage and adjust their approach as needed as students progressed.

A shift into digital learning has been accelerated in the real world with recent events, but leveraging the full advantage and opportunities for tailored learning has yet to be embraced. For now, it seems the student experience will remain "one of many" in a classroom, be it virtual or in person. Imagine the benefit of more individualized learning plans, based on the student's abilities and interests. Teachers would have the means to better support students who need more time with a required subject while enabling other students to accelerate to mastery without downtime or boredom. Tailored learning meets each student where they are and moves their learning forward. It will require investment in new assessments to ensure mastery, in new teaching techniques for a multi-progressive classroom, and a shift to focus on learning and inclusion rather than on grades achieved.

****

For Leadership, understanding and being understood are essential for engagement. Formal and informal leaders are the first test of the Contrast statement; these are the navigators, the leaders of change. If your leaders fail to see the benefit of the change, they will present resistance, pursue other routes, and hinder any movement forward. Take the time to identify leaders, experts, and influencers who have a stake in the change initiative; listen to their perspectives on value to the organization, discuss their concerns, and engage each as a collaborative partner in navigating change.

Now it's time to seal the deal with Experiences that demonstrate and reinforce the Contrast, bringing home the desired change and how to effectively move forward toward success.

E IS FOR EXPERIENCES

"The man who moves a mountain begins by carrying away small stones."

—Confucius, philosopher

If the Contrast statement is the map for the change journey, the Experiences are the engine. Individuals and organizations don't change because they logically see the merit in change; individuals and organizations change because they buy in (see), understand how to change (move), and sustain the changed behavior/process as the recognized standard (adopted). Each of these phases presents an inherent potential failure point—failure to see, failure to move, and failure to adopt.

In the Experience element, we must deliberately architect Experiences to mitigate the failure points for all leaders, doers, and users. Experiences may be events, communications, or programs specific to the project implementing a change. Experiences are also embedded in everyday actions, including feedback, on-the-job training, recognition or promotion announcements, who is recognized in meetings, who attends important meetings, who reports directly to the big boss and who has another layer of management, and so on. We introduce, motivate, and instantiate the change through these deliberate Experiences.

Experience is the biggest factor in the change journey!

Details: Experiences

Early in my career, I was introduced to the writings of Conners, Smith, and Hickman. To paraphrase one of the many gems in their Partners in Leadership programming (2019), the authors suggest a hierarchy of behavior wherein Experiences drive Beliefs, establishing the Culture of an organization. Beliefs then drive Actions, which in turn drive Results. The key to changing Results, therefore, is to change the foundational Experiences in a deliberate and intentional way: Experiences drive Beliefs, which then drive Actions and Results.

As I've presented this concept to clients, the words sometimes create uncomfortable reactions. The term "Beliefs" is too personal; religious; ethereal. Culture (the sum of Experiences and Beliefs) is renamed "Environment" or "Working Philosophy." This is all semantics.

Can a large corporation have Beliefs? Do they have an inherent Culture? I say, "YES."

Using the pyramid, we can discern what needs to change and how to present that change to the individual who must operate differently.

For example, any change requires Action to execute it. If an individual doesn't Believe she can execute the process in the new way the Action requires, the Experiences must take her step by step to build confidence and commitment—without confidence and commitment, she will not Believe and therefore not Act, and the Results will not change.

Change is hard—is there any way to make it easy? Do we know what the new thing is—process, product, behavior? And what is the right way to execute the new thing? All of these questions are tied back to the Contrast statement and the measures of success—you can see why Contrast is the map of the CLEAR Change Method!

We define and implement Experiences to drive new thinking and acceptance, and to build the Beliefs necessary to work differently. With these Beliefs, we can take Action to implement the needed change successfully and accomplish the much-needed Results for the business.

Architect deliberate and meaningful Experiences to answer the following statement:

How can we Make it Easy to Do the New Thing the Right Way?

Experiences fall into several categories, each contributing to the culture of the organization (Galbraith 2014). Use these categories to brainstorm Experiences that make it easy to do the new thing the right way.

- *Processes* define the means or steps by which work is accomplished. The process may be formal and structured, expertise based, or absent. In the first parable, the Duck compared the process of swimming to the process of walking, establishing it was a process and it was somewhat familiar for the Knight. Establishing processes with visual aids makes it easy to execute the process correctly and consistently.
- *People Capability* considers skills or expertise needed to conduct work in the new way. The Knight practiced swimming in the pond, a safe environment, before committing to crossing the raging river. Consider ways to allow for learning and practicing in a safe environment with active coaching to make it easy to move and adopt a new process, product, or behavior.
- *Leadership* behaviors during the change journey create experiences for all to see. As we discussed in the Leadership chapter, this is one of the toughest areas to manage consistently. In the NewBee parable, the EllerBee Queen did not share what she knew of the

Farmer's control on the colony, setting the NewBee colony up for disappointment and destruction. Do you think the Squadron would trust her in the future? With her omission of key facts, the EllerBee Queen destroyed any trust in the colony's culture. Define the expected Leadership behaviors in alignment with your Contrast statement, and recognize those leaders who demonstrate the desired behaviors. Recognition of a leader who does not model desired behaviors will invalidate the desired behaviors quickly; people will behave in accordance to what is rewarded.

- *Governance* describes the business rules and how decisions are made. Governance reflects the operational priorities, defining who and what the organization values. In the Warren parable, any Council member could redirect resources from Eva's project; the intact governance structure did not adjust with the urgency of the situation. Define how to prioritize and rights for decision-making in accordance with desired results and culture.
- *Organizational Structure* defines who reports to whom, organizing resources into areas of responsibility. The organizational structure is a less important factor compared to the others, but it may be a major factor in your change journey. In the NewBees parable, the organizational structure is how the hive survives; it

is essential to their culture. Recognizing the Farmer in their organizational structure would have helped the NewBees understand their options. Consider how your organizational structure communicates priorities, the relative importance of each area of responsibility, and the availability of your leadership team.

- *Technology* is often used to drive change rather than compliment or make the desired change easier. People capability and processes are essential to successful Technology implementation. Although not specifically technology, the Duck used the river's current to guide the Knight to a safe landing spot; the current augmented the Knight's new swimming capability. Look for technology applications to make it easy to do the new thing the right way.

Your change initiative may require many Experiences, delivered over weeks, months, or years; we can capture and prioritize the list in an *Experience Map*. Creating an Experience Map for each affected group organizes the Experiences, pacing, and sequence of the change initiative. Prioritize the list based on the resources available, timing required, and impact needed for each affected group. Finally, be sure to prioritize the Experiences necessary to drive change at the enterprise level; these Experiences are foundational, tied to culture and Beliefs you wish to cultivate across the entire organization.

Intentional planning and execution are necessary, with attention to detail and resources.

Here is an example of an abbreviated Experience Map from the Warren parable, representing Eva's plans for each category; more examples of Experiences are presented in the case studies.

Category	Experience	Target Audience	When
Process	Demonstrate escape tunnels	Randall, Council members, Elders	as soon as available
People Capability	Practice drill for escape (with new tunnels in place)	the Warren as a whole	asap, before the attack
Leadership	1st hand accounting of the attacks and destruction	Randall and Council members	when they arrive
Governance	discussion on priorities and resource availability/ support	Randall	after demo
Org Structure	use Elders in privacy demonstration	Randall and Council members	day 2 (plan)
Technology	Show how sound is muffled, even with escape tunnels (privacy demonstration)	Randall and Council members	as soon as available

As stated earlier, your change initiative may require many Experiences, and it can be a challenge to create a long list with a consistently high impact. An effective Experience:

- Connects to the Contrast statement and Measures of Success
- Promotes learning or understanding of the future state
- Instills confidence in moving to or adopting the future state
- Demonstrates desired behaviors
- Creates memorable moments

Keys for Success: Experiences

- How can we Make it Easy to Do the New Thing the Right Way?
- Experiences are not single events; repetition over time is required to inspire movement and adoption for the long term.

Pitfalls in Experiences

It's easy to lose your way or fall back to old habits, both for those invested in the change and those who are asked to do something new. Here are some common scenarios:

- It's too Hard—I was more efficient doing it "the normal way"

We are creatures of habit. Individuals who are trained or used to doing work in "the normal way" find it difficult to put aside long-standing habits to take on a new process. Consider how you drive to work each day: you know the route, the time it takes, the traffic patterns. When there is construction, another route may be a better choice—but your car seems to drive the normal route. You have to be very deliberate in choosing the alternative route. The same is true with any change. Counter "it's too hard" with "here's how we've made it easier."

Engage your experts and informal leaders in defining how to make the new work easier. Remember, these experts have been rewarded for their expertise in the status quo, often mentoring others to adopt current practices. Experts are essential to defining the new process or product, debugging issues, and teaching others how to do the work differently to deliver on Measures of Success. Create specific Experiences for experts, and they will create aligned Experiences for others.

- Mixed Messages—finding the convenient path

Similar to mixed messages in Leadership, mixed Experiences will set the change initiative back to the starting blocks faster than you can say CLEAR. Imagine you hired a new painting company because they could complete the job faster than your normal vendor. Unfortunately, they showed up with only half of the crew thereby extending the timeline. The benefit you expected was negated; you should have stuck with the normal vendor.

We must consistently present Experiences with a tie back to the Contrast statement, as well as emphasizing commitment to drive the path forward to success. Players who are unsure or resistant to the change will amplify any data that supports the hypothesis of "the old way is better."

Any messages or behaviors that hint at going back or holding back on the change implementation will be recognized quickly, shared widely and discussed loudly by Resistors. Any casual recognition that the old way was preferred, any distraction from the defined path forward, or any hint at reprioritization creates a viable detour for the change-averse. To prevent or mitigate the pitfall of Mixed Messages, each message must clearly align with the Contrast statement, and leaders must consistently deliver these messages with knowledge, authenticity, and commitment—even if they don't personally agree with the change.

- Limited Resources—you can't give what you don't have

If a change requires specific headcount, funding, or capabilities, then the change implementation cannot move forward until these requirements are satisfied or the solution is reworked. If a process requires four workers, implementing with only three workers will inevitably create negative Experiences, evolving into a negative spiral of Beliefs (lack of motivation, feeling ignored or not valued by leadership, thinking that the change isn't worth the time or effort). If, however, the process is reconfigured for three workers, and these workers are developed to operate well (allowed to practice, autonomy for process control, team building), the workers will build confidence, commitment, and Beliefs that support the new process and change initiative. They will then strive to take Action to deliver Results.

Consider what your organization needs and may not have. Examples include capabilities, new technology, diversity of thought, inclusive culture, and so on. Then, discuss long-term investments you can make in Experiences to drive Results.

Avoiding pitfalls in the Experience category is nearly impossible; even the most structured program has unanticipated events that may drive the need for additional communication, adjustment, or improvement. There is risk inherent in any change! We will further explore anticipating risk as we understand Accountability in the next chapter. For now, let's look at some Experience case studies.

****

Case Study 5: More Priestly Practice

Recall Father Brian and the implementation of the revised missal? As Father Brian engaged the parish priests as Leaders, he created important and memorable Experiences as they worked together to understand and implement the change.

As mentioned in Case Study 4, Father Brian gathered small groups of parish priests together for workshops; these workshops were key Experiences, as the parish priests knew each other but rarely worked together as pastoral leaders. During the workshop, Father Brian invited each priest to share his personal connection with celebrating the Mass, creating memorable moments among the priests as they shared. As the group explored the new missal and related changes to common prayers and responses, Father Brian created the opportunity to practice these unfamiliar phrases in a safe learning environment. The priests shared with each other where there were challenges (*consubstantial* may be a hard word to say) and new insights (*and with your spirit* has deep meaning). Father Brian brought up that he valued this reset from rote to conscious response, encouraging reflection and curiosity across parishioners. They would actually think about the words they were saying, rather than just repeating phrases they had memorized. This discussion enabled processing and adoption as a collective and collaborative group. These Experiences brought the parish priests together for shared understanding and support.

Father Brian asked: How might we make it easy for the congregation to do the new thing the right way? The answer: Provide the text for easy reference. Many of the priests incorporated printed worship aids for those who attend mass. The aids highlighted the revised words in red text, with the unchanged text presented in black. By using color coding, it was comforting to note how few words had actually changed—but highlighted the fact that enough words had been changed that it created a new learning Experience.

The worship aids were available to any parish, lessening the burden of implementation without dictating how or when, as each parish priest directed implementation timing based on local needs. The Archdiocese replicated the workshops across an expanded region during the implementation period, creating Experiences which enabled full implementation on or ahead of schedule.

****

Even the most accomplished leaders create Experiences with unintended consequences. Let's review a case study of an exceptional leader who took a wrong turn.

Case Study 6: Talent Dilemma

More than a decade ago, Paige grew tired of commuting across the country for her role with a big corporation and decided it was time to establish her own consulting firm. Paige has significant expertise and a drive to improve customer experience, and was a successful entrepreneur right out the gate.

She now leads a small-yet-mighty company and has been recognized as a "best place to work" for several years running.

A few years ago, Paige was considering stepping back from the more operational elements of her role, allowing her to focus on growth and strategy. As a result, she pursued a search for a new executive-level leader.

Searching for a ready candidate was a departure from the standard recruiting/hiring approach. Typically, Paige's hiring approach focused on an approximately 60 percent technical fit, with a clear cultural fit and desire to learn. In this case, she deliberately deviated and hired a candidate based solely on the technical expertise needed to deliver business outcomes. Unfortunately, the individual hired was not engaged with the culture at all. They showed a lack of flexibility and limited tolerance for less experienced employees—the individual was not a successful fit for the role and exited after three months.

Paige had deviated from a proven process, and in doing so, she and the hired executive created new Experiences for herself and her employees that did not fit the culture. The results were not aligned to Paige's overall strategy and desired culture, thereby not creating desired results. True to her nature, Paige and her team spent several months analyzing the recent executive hiring process and resulting Experiences; the team resolved to hire with a bias for cultural fit for all positions. Paige subsequently focused on recruiting and successfully hiring leaders who were technically strong *and* demonstrated passion, flexibility, and cultural fit, resulting in continued growth in reach and revenue.

****

The Contrast statement is the map for your change initiative, Leadership is the navigation, and Experiences are the engine. Experiences drive Beliefs, establishing the cultural foundation of Actions and Results. A change succeeds or fails due to its Experiences.

Successful leaders deliberately create, deliver, and adjust the Experience Map to resolve issues and move the organization forward. These leaders demonstrate commitment and ownership, defined as Accountability. Let's understand the elements of Accountability to address potential risks and ensure commitment to do the new thing the right way.

A IS FOR ACCOUNTABILITY

"The best way to starve a dog is to ask two people to feed it."

—my dear friend Pam

I'm sure someone else first shared the quip quoted above, but I know it first made an impact on me when my friend Pam shared it in a meeting. Without clear Accountability, architectured Experiences may not be implemented. Assumptions and distractions may rule the day, with potentially devastating results.

Accountability establishes clear roles and ownership for the planned actions and outcomes. Accountability ensures Leadership alignment, execution of Experiences, and progress along the change journey. You must set clear and meaningful expectations of what is to be done, by whom, and by when—otherwise, nothing would get done at all. As we discussed in the previous chapter, Experiences drive Actions—for instance, donating to a charity at a fundraising event. Accountability drives ownership and commitment—leading the fundraising efforts or becoming a member of the charity's board of directors. Let's explore the details of Accountability.

Details: Accountability

"Accountability" has a negative connotation. Holding someone Accountable has a threatening sound to it, often tied to negative consequences. In the CLEAR Change Model, however, Accountability describes personal commitment and credibility—all positive elements! And in that light, we talk about Accountability as ownership, integrity, and perseverance to contribute and lead your share of the work.

To capture Accountability or ownership, the best tool is a standard Action Plan, a document outlining any actions to be completed, by whom, by when. Simple in format, the Action Plan (template below) marshals all the actions—Experiences, communications, issue resolutions, measures of success, celebrations—into an organized plan. Often organized by date, the Action Plan is derived from the Experience Map in the prior chapter. Continuing with the Warren parable, Eva's Action Plan might look as follows:

When	Action Item	Target Audience	Accountable	Status
Day 1	build decoy warren	builder bunnies	Eva	done
Day 2 (plan)	use Elders in privacy demonstration	Randall and Council members	Grandmother	done
Day 3	build example escape tunnels in expansion burrows	builder bunnies	Eva	done
Day 4	Show how sound is muffled, even with escape tunnels (privacy demonstration)	Randall and Council members	Eva	done
Day 4	Demonstrate escape tunnels	Randall, Council members, Elders	Eva	done
Day 4	1st hand accounting of the attacks and destruction	Randall and Council members	Randall	done
Day 4	discussion on priorities and resource availability/ support	Randall	Eva	done
Day 5	build escape tunnels in main Warren	builder bunnies	Eva	done
Day 6	formal warning communication	entire Warren	Randall	done
Day 6	Practice drill for escape (with new tunnels in place)	the Warren as a whole	Randall	in progress

Eva has outlined the work to be accomplished by the builder bunnies each day. She has incorporated the Experience Map items, again arranged by date. As the project manager, Eva has included action items Randall and her Grandmother must complete, recording the status to ensure all activities are completed on time.

The Action Plan should be constructed early in project planning, reviewed regularly to ensure progress and to surface issues. The Action Plan is a communication tool for the implementation team and Leadership. Regular updates, additional action items, and status updates inform progress as well as enable recognition for milestone completions. Action Plans are dynamic documents, supporting the change initiative from early design through full implementation and adoption.

I often hear Accountability and Responsibility used interchangeably; I believe there is an important difference. Responsibility is an agreement to take on an assignment and see it through to completion. Accountability is the authority and commitment to the completion of the assignment, including assignment of resources, resolving issues, and making decisions as needed. The responsible individual asks "what can I do to help?" where the accountable individual says "we must do better," finds the resources, and moves forward.

In the Warren parable, Eva was responsible for implementing the protection plan, leading the builders in constructing the decoy warren and escape routes. Randall, the head rabbit, was accountable for the safety of the Warren. He accepted Eva's plan, granting her the responsibility to implement, while he continued to evaluate other options. Randall was ready to negotiate relocation to another Warren if Eva's plan did not work, building contingency plans and accepting the possibility his community may be destroyed beyond repair.

It's a subtle difference, and if everything is going well, the only difference is who throws the party (the accountable leader). However, if issues arise, the accountable leader must drive to eliminate the barriers and resolve issues, getting the plan back on track

Keys for Success: Accountability

- A defined Action Plan organizes the work that is necessary to drive the intended change, including Experiences, Measures of Success, and Reinforcement activities (next chapter).
- Proactively identify Risks and incorporate them into the Action Plan accordingly (see Pitfalls section).

Pitfalls in Accountability

To deliver with Accountability, we must define and address risk.

For a change initiative, the work can be exhausting. It is much easier to repeat what we have always done than it is to change to something new, no matter how small the shift. For those in charge, the commitment to lead a change initiative adds to their burden. A targeted and specific review of risks, along with recommended actions to address these risks, helps to reduce the burden with organized plans.

Reflecting back to the Leadership chapter, the formal or informal leaders who have positive scores for Interest, Influence, and Impact are obvious choices as Accountable leaders for key elements. For some change initiatives, these assignments will work wonders.

We also recognize there are Leaders who are neutral or resistant to the change, who may be looking to enable shortcuts or detours along the path. The Accountability phase calls for a proactive identification of these shortcuts, as heard through formal and informal channels.

Risk Assessment begins by asking questions.

Risks can be negative, resulting in pain. For these risks, ask:

- What could go Wrong?
- What might Break?
- How could we "Cheat," taking unproven or unwanted shortcuts?
- What happens Downstream (that could break, go wrong, be overwhelmed by our supply)?
- What happens Upstream (that could cause us to break, go wrong, starve our supply)?
- How often does each painful issue occur? All the time, some of the time, or rarely?

Risks also can be positive, presenting advantage. For these risks, ask:

- What could be Outstanding?
- How might we Accelerate?
- What happens Downstream (if we are outstanding or accelerate)?

- What happens Upstream (to feed outstanding or accelerated performance)?
- How often does each advantageous event occur? All the time, some of the time, or rarely?

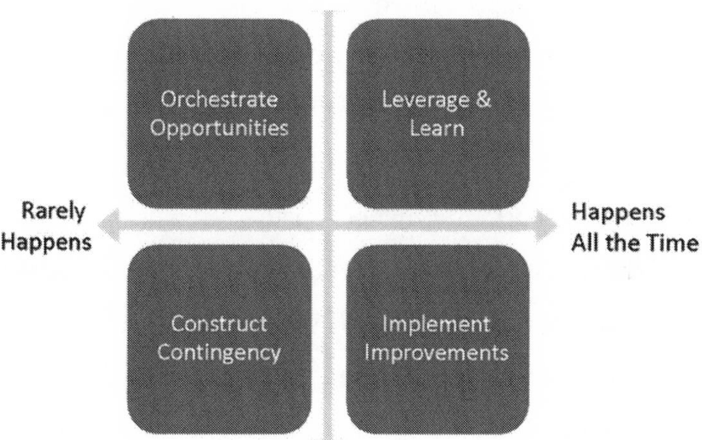

Map the Risk Assessment of Pain or Advantage against the frequency of occurrence. For each combination, develop an appropriate Action to address the Risk. An example is depicted here in our Risk Assessment Grid:

More specifically:

- Leverage and Learn to anticipate and replicate situations that present an advantage and could happen frequently. These are best-case scenarios for rapid growth and change. Examples include five-star reviews, high-performing territories, products with a higher competitive position.

- Implement Improvements for recurring painful issues. Informal leaders and the workers most impacted by the change are best positioned to identify issues and work to improve the process or service. In many cases, improvement projects are Experiences tied to the change initiative. Examples include waste reduction, root-cause evaluation to resolve complaints, new product features to address issues.
- Construct Contingency plans for painful issues that may not occur frequently, if at all. Planning for the worst-case scenario is essential to responding quickly, should the situation arise. Examples include succession planning, tornado-recovery planning, system-outage recovery, back-up files.
- Orchestrate Opportunities by creating opportunities for positive advantage. Because these opportunities may not happen organically, proactive planning and orchestration may be necessary. Examples include planning for explosive sales/uptake, special offers, free templates in exchange for your email address.

Risk Assessment and proactive Action Planning drive both confidence and Accountability. Addressing negative issues as well as creating positive scenarios facilitates change implementation and success. In addition, Risk Assessment and Action Planning engage Leadership to own and deliver the desired business outcomes to realize the Contrast statement and ultimate success.

****

The following case study shows how to Implement Improvements.

Case Study 7: Collaborative Forms

Jan is a vibrant customer care manager working for a regional not-for-profit that supports individuals with progressive illnesses. State and local agencies recently recognized the organization for excellent patient and family care, specifically their wellness programs.

Newly proposed legislation at the state level would require wellness programming in local hospitals. Jan's organization is well-positioned to provide the required services as a partner to local hospitals. This line of business offered high growth and a consistent stream of income for the organization, which was clearly aligned with their mission to promote patient quality of life. Jan was tasked with growing the infrastructure in anticipation of high growth in patient visits, including using a new database for patient records and ease of access for the patient and family members.

When we met Jan, she was very competent at data entry and responsive to those patients who showed up at the front door but were not in the system. However, the not-for-profit's volunteers entered the information on the fly, with only the basic information captured and not always checked for duplication. They did not always tie family members to the qualifying patient, and at times, there was not an accurate record of who had come through the doors for popular wellness programs.

Jan was feeling the pain every day, but she was the only one. Clear accounting of visitors (patients and family members) would be necessary for reimbursement, compliance reporting, and future grants based on volume of patients served. Jan needed an easy way to enter the constant stream of data into the system. She needed accurate and complete data that could be recalled for program registration and attendance. Nobody else understood the difficulties in managing patient data.

As we walked the process for data acquisition and entry, we noticed a number of collated stacks of paper on Jan's desk. Each stack was a collection of forms, sent daily from the nursing contacts at each hospital, providing information for prospective patients to be entered into the system. Patients were then, through the system, invited to visit. Great! The nurses were the primary contact with the patients, providing accurate and timely data; we just had to figure out how to get it into the system.

Jan sorted and stacked papers because each form was different—different format, different information, different notations. They were all, furthermore, different from the fields/format necessary for data entry. Engaging the nurses to connect patients more directly to the wellness programming was a great idea, but they had put no thought to how the information would flow.

We asked, "How can we Make it Easy for the Nurses to Provide the Right Information in the Right Format for easy data entry?" Here's what we learned:

- Nurse Navigators were using forms they had been used to using for other service connections. They were used to paper, and fill-in-the-blank was the most-used mode.
- Jan had a clear picture of what information she needed for each patient. She often didn't receive the data she needed or received a lot of information she didn't need.
- Eliminating data fields would appeal to the nurses and their commitment to data privacy.
- Jan had invested time with the database support technician; she could rearrange the data fields on her entry screen if necessary.
- A direct feed from the hospital system into the organization's system would take time and resources, with privacy concerns as a potential show-stopper.

With this information, Jan held workshops with the nurses from each hospital to engage them in the process for patient registration and invitation to wellness programs. She shared her patient tracking system, including what were required data fields, how the data were used for invitation, registration, and attendance at programs. Jan also explained the use of the anonymized data for state and grant-based reports. These Experiences helped the nurses understand how data was used and why certain fields were necessary. Finally, Jan shared the varied data forms she was receiving from each hospital, where data was missing, and what information she would sometimes receive that she did not need. Jan then asked the nurses to design one data collection form that made sense for all of them to use; she used their expertise in engaging with the patients to gather the information in the most effective way for the patient. With the new format, Jan then mirrored the data collection form on her data entry screen for ease of use.

By engaging the nurses, Jan aligned to the needs of the patient, simplified her process, and could now delegate the data-entry process for daily updates in a fraction of the time. In addition, she created a partnership Experience with the nurses, reinforcing their shared focus on patient wellness and care. Although not a big impact on resources or funding, the streamlined process ensured a welcoming experience for patients and family members as they walked into the door—it told them, "We know you, and you are welcome."

****

A case study showing failure in Accountability is difficult to admit and even more difficult to document. This one hits particularly close to home.

Case Study 8: Can you hear me now?

In the decade following the 9/11 attacks on the US, the growing need to define employment status via access to systems or facilities coalesced into a business requirement to efficiently and consistently identify, manage, and grant access to contracted employees. Across corporations of medium to large size, the challenge to categorize and manage contracted employees reflected the outsourcing trend of recent years. There were multiple employment categories, multiple access points, and even worse, multiple contract supervisors; creating a robust process to manage all of these different categories would not be simple, and it would not be easy to implement. Every business leader relied on contracted resources as a flexible workforce, and very few considered it necessary to differentiate contracted employees from corporate employees—even though the US Government required differentiation for tax purposes. It was a courtesy (and it was easy) to manage contracted employees the same as corporate employees, especially when it came to system access, facilities access, communications, services, etc.

The US government was interested in a clear delineation of workforce categories to ensure wages, benefits, and taxes were paid appropriately. At the same time, corporations were learning of security issues, both physical and intellectual, with the burgeoning threat of what we now know as cybersecurity on the horizon. The Leadership tasked my group with defining a system to capture, manage, and integrate access permissions for contracted employees globally.

We opted to employ a contracted software system to catalog and manage our contracted workforce. I had a marvelous team of Accountable and passionate leaders who resolved several challenges along this significant change journey. We integrated the best-in-class software for facility and systems access management, tested scenarios, established a governance committee to resolve issues, defined risk scenarios and action plans, leveraged focus groups to refine communications and deployed on schedule—great, right?

In the US, the model relied on the supervisor, the individual who had Accountability for the funding, staffing, and work conducted by any contracted resource. The software, also designed in the US, delivered supervisor-driven processing with minimal delegation—an issue to be resolved in future enhancements. We decided to launch with this supervisor-only execution design, providing education and helpdesk support until the delegation model would allow for consolidation into administrative assistant roles. This approach aligned well with the self-service model for HR and financial services that had recently been deployed across the US.

Our colleagues in our larger affiliates, primarily in Europe, had concerns. Most notably, they shared concerns related to supervisor capability, the different levels of approvals that would be necessary, and the differing definitions—multiplicity of definitions, actually—of "contracted resources" in local parlance. We didn't hear them. We thought they just disagreed with our approach. Given the right education and experiences, we believed the supervisors would come up the curve. Afterall, we thought, most supervisors have the same assigned accountabilities in their roles, and we were helping them do their job more efficiently with technology. We were really wrong.

We launched the system and felt great about it all; we had addressed an emerging need with a novel approach, and it was working. Until the next evening, when it went live in Europe. The trouble tickets, emails, voicemails, and chats from EU colleagues were mounting rapidly; they were overwhelmed. Supervisors across Europe didn't understand what they were to do, how to do it, or how to get help. Contracted manufacturing employees could not gain access to the facility or essential systems. Our colleagues in Europe were in the middle of a leadership tornado, and we had created it. Furthermore, the Accountability for all aspects of contracted workers did not reside with the supervisor at all. In Europe, the Accountability resided with the HR team for the affiliate, the very same friends and colleagues who had raised concerns months ago. Our failure was in understanding Accountability and how we had assigned roles within the contractor management system; we assumed and assigned Accountability to the supervisor who could not take action, and we did not provide access to the HR partners who were truly accountable.

As I mentioned, I was fortunate to have an excellent team. We were Accountable for the overall system and had made assumptions that created serious issues. We stepped back, partnered to establish country-by-country plans to provide access and support to the HR teams, and worked to mend relationships. We listened to requirements, established more specific definitions based on local workforce strategies, and expanded access assignment options with the software vendor. The change initiative moved forward, and we benefited in the long-term from having the system in place; strategic partnerships on specific drug products were enabled readily for new relationships and dissolved promptly as the agreements expired. The miss on Accountability and Leadership created learning for all of us.

****

The plan is in place—you're done, right? You've defined your Contrast statement and defined success; the Leadership team is on board or at least neutral; you've mapped and planned Experiences with clear Accountability and risk-response plans. Hooray! Let's implement!

Hold your horses. We have one last thing to discuss.

This is where the hard part really sets in. The exciting part is over, and the long slog into uncertainty has begun. You and your team will get tired, so very tired, and you may even start asking yourself, "Why are we doing this, anyway?"

The last step in the process is perhaps the most important. Let's learn how to remember why we are doing this in the first place, even when the going gets tough, with Reinforcement and Reward.

R IS FOR REINFORCEMENT (AND REWARD)

"What gets recognized gets reinforced, and what gets reinforced gets repeated."

—Unknown

Reinforcement and Reward along the journey are key to long-term adoption. It's not just about the ultimate goal or outcome. Celebrating interim milestones, progress toward implementation, and progress toward desired outcomes help drive your team across the finish line!

Communication of progress, milestones, and outcomes reminds Leadership of the Contrast statement, the priority, and the value of the change. Reinforcing the From—To and Why, as well as recognizing progress to Measures of Success and encouraging continued commitment along the journey all help everyone accept and adopt the new normal, sustaining the desired change.

Details: Reinforcement

You've made the case for change, and most players are at least trying the new path forward—but will they stick with it? History would suggest they will not; only 28 percent of change initiatives deliver on the expected results (Jacquemont, Maor and Reich 2019). Many initiatives fail because we get tired, lost, or disinterested—or perhaps because the next change initiative has already been launched!

Reinforcement, reward, and recognition are all integral elements on the journey of change. As we've stated before, change is hard. Arduous. Challenging. Tiring. When the new process is difficult at the beginning and still difficult after rounds of practice, the old process looks very appealing—even if the change to the new process is critical to company survival. Recognition of minor accomplishments along the way, taking time to reflect how much progress has been made, and recommitment to the ultimate goal will energize a tired team, enable progress, and encourage discretionary effort to fully adopt the change.

Reinforcement includes recognition of intermediate milestones and celebrating the early wins. By recognizing milestones, you validate the accomplishments of those who are engaged. You also establish value for the effort and the Contrast statement (helpful for the undecided), and you create a contrary experience for those entrenched in the past. Reinforcement requires planning, including progress tracking in defined segments or phases. For each phase, Leadership must establish measures of success and expectations, with realistic yet challenging goals aligned with the successful outcomes as defined in the Contrast statement.

Reinforcement also includes recognition of individual effort or accomplishment. Delivering something the team or individual values yields the best result. In any organization, how Leadership behaves, rewards others, and is rewarded, are key Experiences visible in the community. Who is recognized, for what actions or accomplishments—flavored by the veracity of that recognition—speaks more loudly than any trinket, award, or thank you speech. Recognition and promotion of the desired behaviors must be defined clearly, followed religiously, and communicated authentically; any perceived deviation will be taken as reinforcement of new (or worse yet, old) behaviors, requiring significant effort to correct course.

Above all, Reinforcement provides an opportunity to recall the Contrast elements: From-To, Why, and Measures of Success. You Reinforce the value with each milestone or early win, building a series of achievements tied directly to the Contrast statement. In this way, Reinforcement builds momentum to accomplish the defined Measures of Success, with celebrated progress along the journey. Only with defined Measures of Success can we understand when we have actually adopted our change!

Keys for Success: Reinforcement

- Reinforcement relies on defined milestones and Measures of Success.
- Reinforcement is the opportunity to recall the Contrast statement, communicate progress, and encourage adoption.

Pitfalls in Reinforcement

The biggest pitfall in the Reinforcement element is not doing it at all. Measures of Success may be difficult to define, with interim milestones presenting an added challenge. This is why Measures of Success are *required* in the Contrast element! Only with Measures of Success can we mark progress and accurately declare victory. Similarly, we orchestrate Reinforcement opportunities with established progress-evaluation points, natural milestones, or implementation phases. These are projected points in time to reflect on the progress, recognize accomplishments, and reinforce the change initiative's reason for existing: the Contrast Statement.

Similarly, neglecting to share milestones, progress, or accomplishments with the invested Leadership team is common. In the Leadership element, we captured formal and informal leaders with interest, influence, and impact on the change initiative. Reinforcement includes communication to the invested Leadership and those impacted by the change. Not all leaders are living with the change initiative or project as closely as you and your team, so they'd benefit from formal updates. Regularly scheduled communication provides the opportunity to orchestrate support while Reinforcing the Contrast statement, Measures of Success, and progress toward adoption.

The remaining pitfall is the Shiny Object Syndrome, wherein the Leadership becomes distracted by another big idea. This distraction often manifests as the next important challenge or new priorities, impatiently discussed before realizing the benefits of the current change already underway. Shiny Object Syndrome hits after we reach a significant milestone or perhaps when the Contrast statement and Strategic Plan have become rote, boring, last year's news. In this case, the Leadership team itself needs Reinforcement.

Change is challenging for everyone, even the very Leaders who are sponsoring the initiative! Intentional planning for Reinforcement of the Why, Measures of Success, and desired impact is key to remaining on track for adoption of any change. Let's look at case studies to explore the importance of intentional Reinforcement.

Case Study 9: We Are Family

Marty leads a growing firm that specializes in individual insurance and financial services across the Midwest. Typical for this industry, Marty's firm employs a small staff with most of the workforce operating as independent advisors under contract. Marty has grown the firm substantially, with a number of key acquisitions and expansions in the past decade. Multiple states have recognized the firm as one of the "Best Places to Work." Marty treats the firm as a family, with a deliberate eye on culture as a key element of successful business.

Marty admits their Measures of Success have not always been so rosey. In their 2005 assessment, the firm's corporate partner ranked them in the lowest quartile of performance. In a strategic move, Marty defined the future state as achieving a top 10 performance ranking. Amazingly, the firm achieved Top 10 performance recognition in 2010—just five years later—and has retained this level of high performance ever since.

How did he do it?

First, Marty defined his Contrast statement, linking the performance gain from bottom quartile to Top 10 with specific measures for increased revenue and advisors under contract. The Why was to serve their clients by facilitating individualized investment strategies (and making money along the way). Marty communicated clear Measures of Success, refreshed each year based on the performance achieved.

Second, Marty leveraged market consolidation trends to acquire offices in neighboring states. Each office was performing at a lower production rate. Marty set clear expectations on performance and growth to align and integrate the new associates. He continued to encourage and reinforce expectations for high financial performance in the home office. As the frequency of acquisitions accelerated, the key challenge was to leverage new growth potential while not compromising culture or productivity.

Through it all, Marty consistently reinforced the family culture. Where possible, Marty would visit newly acquired offices to welcome the team into the family and share his perspectives and expectations. He communicated measured improvement goals tailored to that office's capabilities and surrounding market. Marty formed swat teams of leaders to carry his message, creating shared ownership across the leadership team. It was essential to welcome each office in person and have a consistent leadership presence, messaging, and exchange of concerns with direct access to Marty.

Marty's *Advisor First* culture reflects how he expects his advisors to treat customers, citing strong correlation to the successful performance of the business. Marty and his leadership team spend time on what some leaders would consider fluff activities: family-oriented company events; annual photo books; recognition programs; and dedicated time for 1:1 discussion. Regular Reinforcement of identity and alignment with the firm—being part of the family—buffers the uncertainty of a changing industry environment. This culture, formed from specific Experiences, made it easy for engaged and high-performing advisors to remain under contract.

Finally, Marty consistently drives for results. He clearly communicates the expectations for each office and each individual. The culture focuses on family, but in Marty's family, everyone contributes. He sets clear expectations for leadership, with three consistent principles: serve our customers, support our advisors, and be accessible to staff and each other. Marty challenges his sales managers and senior advisors to develop and coach each newer advisor to grow into a high performing player. And he challenges every location to leverage the same systems and processes to ensure consistent measures, creating a level playing field for performance goals. Finally, the Measures of Success for the firm are straightforward and ever-present: grow revenue and develop advisors so we can continue to perform at the highest levels, improving on the Top 10 ranking each year. Consistent Reinforcement of key measures, recognition for accomplishments, and relentless focus on the Contrast statement have resulted in Top 10 performance, accolades from corporate partners, and enviable revenue growth year after year. Way to go, Marty!

****

Now let's look at a case study where phased milestones and Reinforcement would have improved the outcome.

Case Study 10: Go Big or Go Home

As the newly promoted leader of a manufacturing site, Kelly was energized by the opportunity for new lines of business to generate revenue. In his first 90 days, he invested in learning the plant processes, employees, and customers, along with the financial statements. The headquarters was overseas; interference would be minimal, but expectations were high, as his plant was supplying all of North America. The potential upside for growth was substantial.

As Kelly studied operations, he noted two key issues: operational performance to plan was substandard because of a high reject rate, and resources for development were often redirected to solve the production issues, therefore causing rejections. To deliver on the growth plan, performance needed to improve.

Kelly established his strategic plan with a solid Contrast statement: Performance would move From substandard To the accolade of Top Performing Site in order to deliver high-quality product on schedule. Kelly established Measures of Success as percentage on-time to schedule, percentage of first-time quality and growth in number of customers and revenue. He set the performance goals at Top Performing Site levels, well known across the corporation. Kelly was clear and decisive, and his leadership team was committed to moving forward.

Kelly had seen adoption of the Lean Six Sigma process improvement methodology produce strong results in his prior company, specifically in variability reduction and waste elimination. Kelly enrolled himself with several of his technical and operational leaders into a local Lean Six Sigma training program. As a requirement of the program, each participant was to complete a project in his/her work area, actively coached by the training leader. Once training was complete, Kelly could assign additional projects to further improve operations. Kelly jumped in with both feet, setting his improvement plans into motion.

In his zeal, Kelly committed to 15 concurrent improvement projects. He also committed to development of three new product lines with his development team. After all, the process improvement projects would reduce production issues, allowing the development team plenty of time to innovate.

At the end of the quarter, Kelly reported his plan to headquarters: he communicated the 15 projects and three new product lines in development with key customer research for targeted growth. His superiors were elated, but Kelly's leadership team was unusually subdued. The commitments were overwhelming, the production issues and reject rates were elevated, not lessened, and the production schedule was changing with every shift.

Kelly tried to bolster the leadership team's morale. He reinforced the value of future customer growth and continued to reinforce the importance of the improvement projects for their future success. He committed to spending time with each improvement team to reinforce the value of their project.

As Kelly tried to meet with each improvement team, he quickly realized the impact of launching so many teams concurrently. Each team met only once per week, but many of the experienced employees were on multiple teams; they were in the conference room more often than they were on the manufacturing floor. Novice employees were stretched to cover manufacturing, and many could not anticipate issues or make decisions in a timely fashion; product issues and rejections mounted while confidence declined.

Instead of creating a culture of self-reliance, Kelly had created doubt, unanswered questions, and a lack of support. They had replaced the culture of employee development with reactive response. Measures of Success were tanking, and the general feeling was dejection and surrender. The future was unattainable. The year-end report to headquarters was sadly disappointing, with no progress in operational performance, product development, or customer/revenue growth.

Because *everything* was seen as critically important, *nothing* could be accomplished. Without sequencing improvement projects into implementation phases, there was little opportunity for milestone accomplishment and reinforcement. Without interim measures of success, the distance to the long-term goal appeared out of reach and unreasonable. If Kelly had defined deliberate phases of two to three projects with specific milestones and measures, the early accomplishments would have fueled momentum for subsequent phases. Kelly would have realized progressive improvements on a shorter timeline, with fewer resources, and with limited disruption to his manufacturing operation. Comprehensive change requires planning with deliberate pacing, sequencing, and Reinforcement.

****

Reinforcement is the fuel that sustains us through the long journey of change. Experiences combined with recognition and reward are motivational, reminding us the journey is worth the effort. Recognition of interim milestones provides Leadership the opportunity to Reinforce the Contrast statement, progress toward defined success, and renew assignments and Accountability to deliver the next phase. The CLEAR Change Method, which outlines the elements needed to successfully implement strategic change, is now complete!

CONCLUSION

"Change is the law of life. And those who look only to the past and present are certain to miss the future."

—John F. Kennedy, 35th President of the United States

Leading change in your organization is a big task. Most leaders who take up the mantle of change do not succeed. However, using the CLEAR Change Method can make it easy for you to succeed. The CLEAR Change Method maps the journey, energizes your team, and rewards your progress along the way.

Let's review the five elements and keys for success:

C is for Contrast	**Define the change to be realized** Define where you are, where you are going, and why • Be authentic, be logical, and be realistic From + To + Why = Defined Success • Establish Measures of Success that align with the Contrast statement and the business reality
L is for Leadership	**Engage formal and informal leaders** Understand who is with you and who cares • Take the time to be comprehensive in your Leadership list • Engage Leaders in ongoing discussions to build support and consider concerns
E is for Experiences	**Architect experiences for all** Align every Experience to where you are going and why • How can we Make it Easy to Do the New Thing the Right Way? • Experiences are not single events; repetition over time is required to inspire movement and adoption for the long term
A is for Accountability	**Establish clear roles and ownership** Write down who is doing what and when • A defined Action Plan organizes the work necessary to drive change, including Experiences, Communications, Measures, and Celebrations • Proactively identify Risks and incorporate into the Action Plan accordingly
R is for Reinforcement	**Reinforce the desired outcomes** Communicate the path and progress early and often, reinforcing where you are going and why • Reinforcement relies on defined milestones and Measures of Success • Reinforcement is the opportunity to recall the Contrast statement, communicate progress, and encourage adoption

As for pitfalls, there are too many to list briefly here. If we think through the failure modes, we can address or accept the majority of issues:

- Failure to See: the desired change is not understood or valued
- Failure to Move: individuals have difficulty moving to the future state; they don't know how to act differently or can't break free of the current state
- Failure to Adopt: change is abandoned due to fatigue, loss of interest, or loss of perceived value

We have each experienced failure in some aspect of our career; it is important to remember that failure is not the end point—it's what you do next that matters. Accepting the fact that failure will be part of your change journey is liberating. Anticipate, mitigate, address as much as you can, then have a plan for how you will react, adapt, and respond when failure calls.

You've read the stories of leaders who have led change with great success, and many who have learned important lessons along the way. Take on extraordinary challenges, modeling your Contrast statement after Ethan's as he moved his school from grades to learning and mastery. Connect and engage your Leaders with memorable Experiences as Father Brian did with the parish priests across his region. Understand Accountability and address risks like Jan, creating a collaborative solution to a growing pain point. And remember to Reinforce change at milestones along the journey, as Marty did with his family culture, recalling the Contrast statement and rewarding Measures of Success.

As you practice the CLEAR Change Method, you will create your own Experiences and formulate your own Beliefs to get your own Results. You can accomplish great things, move mountains, create disruption, and change minds.

The path is now CLEAR, so go forth and write your own story!

WORKS CITED

Connors, Roger, Tom Smith, and Craig R. Hickman. The Oz Principle: *Getting Results through Individual and Organizational Accountability*. New York, NY: Portfolio, 2010.

Galbraith, Jay R. "The Star Model." JayGalbraith.com, 2014. https://www.jaygalbraith.com/images/pdfs/StarModel.pdf.

Jacquemont, David, Dana Maor, and Angelika Reich. "How to Beat the Transformation Odds." McKinsey & Company. McKinsey & Company, July 8, 2019. https://www.mckinsey.com/business-functions/organization/our-insights/how-to-beat-the-transformation-odds.

Kotter, John P. *Leading Change*. Boston, MA: Harvard Business Review Press, 2012.

Partners in Leadership. "The Power of The Results Pyramid: Achieving Sustainable Culture Change." Culture Management Experts, December 5, 2019. https://www.partnersinleadership.com/insights-publications/the-power-of-the-results-pyramid-achieving-sustainable-culture-change/.

SPECIAL THANKS

My deepest love to my darling husband, Bob. You have put up with my insecurities, pushed me to think bigger, and been my greatest advocate. From the first time we compared CD collections, alphabetized by artist, I knew we were meant to be together. With this journey and in life, you are my partner and better half. You are red to my blue, calm to my storm, E to my I. I love that you make me laugh every day! I am yours, always.

Love and appreciation to our children: Tommy, Ryan, Carson, and JP. You are people of strong character, and we are so very proud of you all. I thank you for being proud of me as I wrote this book; and thank you for putting up with me as I monopolized the family video calls with the latest details!

Thanks to my sister Sandy, my debate partner, my major-me who can debate every element of this book with more experience and finesse than I can. Thanks for all of the weekday morning pep-talks, feedback, and reminders of "who my people are."

Thanks to my good friend Pam Hrubey for providing a great quote and years of friendship.

Thanks and love to all of my Zionsville friends; your confidence and encouragement helped me move forward, even when I wasn't sure there was a book worth pursuing. Thank you for the cheers, happy hours, and spring break discussions along the journey!

A special thanks to Sandy Graef, teacher and friend extraordinaire, who taught me how to plan my next vacation while on vacation, and how to live & love out loud.

Tons of thanks to each and every leader I interviewed, who will remain anonymous. You will always be close colleagues and dear friends to me. Your openness to map against my model gave me confidence, your candor in sharing "learning events" gave my model credibility. I respect your leadership and commitment to your business.

Thank you to the Self-Publishing School, especially my coach, Brett Hiker; thank you for being positive and supportive, even when I was over-analyzing or being too engineering-like!

Finally, a note of gratitude to my Grandmother, Elsie Mae Freed Bouvé (1893-1991), who lived life on her own terms, served others with love and expertise, appreciated the art of conversation, and ever so softly made her point years before she had the right to vote. Thank you for being a model of independence, etiquette, and grace.

ABOUT THE AUTHOR

Alison Spoonmore is the founder and president of Sabbatical Solutions, Inc, a firm focused on providing executives with support to realize their strategic goals in the areas of change leadership, implementation planning, and programmatic process improvement. Alison's connection to leaders and their organization's culture is reflected in her writing. When she is not writing, Alison consults with executive leaders across industries, including pharmaceuticals, manufacturing, start-ups, higher education, and not-for-profits. With

30+ years of experience, she has enjoyed an 82% success rate in change leadership. In her off-screen life, Alison's passions include baking, watching movies with her husband Bob, and walking their lazy dog, ironically named Nike.

For information about Sabbatical Solutions, visit our website, www.sabbaticalsolutions.com

For more information about CLEAR Change, visit our website, www.ClearChangeBook.com or email contact@clearchangebook.com

Thank You For Reading My Book!

I really appreciate all of your feedback, especially how you have applied the CLEAR Change method in your organization.

Please leave me an honest review on Amazon, letting me know what you thought of the book.

Thanks so much!

Alison